Immigrant Neighbors among Us

Immigrant Neighbors among Us

Immigration across Theological Traditions

EDITED BY

M. Daniel Carroll R.

AND

Leopoldo A. Sánchez M.

PICKWICK *Publications* · Eugene, Oregon

IMMIGRANT NEIGHBORS AMONG US
Immigration across Theological Traditions

Copyright © 2015 Wipf and Stock Publishers. All rights reserved. Except for brief
quotations in critical publications or reviews, no part of this book may be repro-
duced in any manner without prior written permission from the publisher. Write:
Permissions. Wipf and Stock Publishers, 199 W. 8th Ave., Suite 3, Eugene, OR 97401.

Pickwick Publications
An Imprint of Wipf and Stock Publishers
199 W. 8th Ave., Suite 3
Eugene, OR 97401

www.wipfandstock.com

ISBN 13: 978-1-62564-376-6

Cataloguing-in-Publication Data

Immigrant neighbors among us : immigration across theological traditions / edited
by M. Daniel Carroll R. and Leopoldo A. Sánchez M.

xxii + 140 p. ; 23 cm. Includes bibliographical references.

ISBN 13: 978-1-62564-376-6

1. Emigration and immigration—Religious aspects—Christianity. I. Title.

HD6305 F55 I65 2015

Manufactured in the U.S.A.   09/10/2015

A los inmigrantes de nuestras familias, iglesias y comunidades,
Quienes han enriquecido de tantas maneras nuestras vidas y teología.

To the immigrants in our families, churches, and communities,
Who have enriched in so many ways our lives and theology.

Contents

Contributors

Sammy G. Alfaro (PhD, Fuller Theological Seminary), Assistant Professor of Theology at Grand Canyon University, Phoenix, AZ.

M. Daniel Carroll R. (Rodas) (PhD, University of Sheffield), Distinguished Professor of Old Testament at Denver Seminary, Denver, CO, and adjunct professor at El Seminario Teológico Centroamericano, Guatemala City, Guatemala.

Hugo Magallanes (PhD, Drew University), Associate Professor of Christianity and Cultures and Director of the Center for the Study of Latino/a Christianity and Religions at Perkins School of Theology—Southern Methodist University, Dallas, TX.

Juan Francisco Martínez (PhD, Fuller Theological Seminary), Vice Provost, Professor of Hispanic Studies and Pastoral Leadership, and Academic Director of the Center for the Study of Hispanic Church and Community at Fuller Theological Seminary, Pasadena, CA.

Carmen M. Nanko–Fernández (DMin, Catholic University of America), Associate Professor of Hispanic Theology and Ministry and Director of the Hispanic Theology and Ministry Program at the Catholic Theological Union, Chicago, IL.

Rubén Rosario Rodríguez (PhD, Princeton Theological Seminary), Associate Professor of Systematic Theology, Director of the Master of Arts Program in Theological Studies, and Director of the Mev Puleo Scholarship Program in Latin American Politics, Theology, and Culture at Saint Louis University, St. Louis, MO.

Leopoldo A. Sánchez M. (Merino) (PhD, Concordia Seminary), Associate Professor of Systematic Theology, Director of the Center for Hispanic Studies, and The Werner R. H. Krause and Elizabeth Ringger Krause Endowed Chair for Hispanic Ministries at Concordia Seminary, St. Louis, MO.

Foreword

Juan Francisco Martínez

THIS YEAR WILL MARK the fiftieth anniversary of the landmark *Immigration and Nationality Act of 1965* (signed into law in the United States that year on October 3). This legislation provided for more immigration from Asia and legally acknowledged the migratory flows that had already been coming from Latin America. It also placed a strong emphasis on family reunification. Though its sponsors stated that it would not create any changes in the ethnic makeup of the population of the U.S., in fact it changed the face of U.S. migration and the U.S. population in general. It took a while for the impact to be noticed, but by the 1990s it had become clear that the demographic makeup of the country was changing.

The 1965 legislation addressed problems of the past, but it did not create an adequate means for "future flow," namely the new immigrants who would be attracted by economic opportunities or would be pushed out of their countries by civil wars (such as Central Americans) or other people fleeing violence. They were not accounted for in that law. In 1986 Ronald Reagan signed the *Immigration Reform and Control Act* that provided amnesty for millions who were living in the U.S. as undocumented aliens, but again the law did not provide a way for new migrant workers to enter the country legally. During the 1990s the Clinton administration tried to control future flow by reinforcing the U.S.-Mexican border. And September 11, 2001 created a new fear of immigrants, such that more legislation was approved to reinforce the southern border (even though none of the 9/11 terrorists entered from the south, and no known terrorist has ever entered the U.S. through that border).

Throughout the first decade of the twenty-first century there were several attempts to pass another immigration reform law to deal with a new generation of undocumented people in the country, today estimated to be between 11 to 12 million people. All legislative efforts have fallen short, even though polls demonstrate that the majority of people in the U.S. are in favor of comprehensive immigration reform that would legalize the status of these people. The stalemate is such that in November 2014 President Obama proposed a series of executive actions that would provide short-term protection for some of the undocumented. At the time of writing this foreword, the executive order was being challenged in the courts.

Recent attempts to address the reality of these millions of undocumented people in the U.S. sets the framework for this book. Though migration is a global phenomenon, this collection of essays focuses on the United States. Migration is part of the national fabric and is imbedded in its national myths. But historically the immigrant myth represented in the text of "The New Colossus" on the Statue of Liberty has only applied to immigrants from Europe. Migrants from Asia or Latin America did not come by Ellis Island, so they have not been part of the understanding of the U.S. as a country of immigrants. Yet the fastest growing ethnic demographics in the U.S. are Asians and Latinos, both by migration and by birth rates.

Throughout its history the United States has periodically changed its immigration laws depending on the economic, political, and social interests of this country or the sentiments of U.S. citizens toward immigrants. The current situation is similar yet also very different, because of the changing demographic face of the country. There are already many places in the country where the majority of kindergarten students are not of northern European background. The U.S. Census Bureau estimates that sometime during the decade of 2040 the majority of the U.S. population will be part of a "minority" group, something that seems to always loom in the background of any conversation on migration reform. The fact that Congress and the president have not been able to approve new legislation to address this issue demonstrates its complexity and also the contradictory perspectives held by the political leaders of the country.

Christian leaders and churches have been concerned about this situation for many years. This book brings together authors that represent various theological and ecclesial traditions, demonstrating how their particular theological framing addresses the issue of immigrants around the world and of the undocumented in the U.S. in particular. Each author focuses on the "normative" authorities of their tradition (such as encyclicals, key leaders, or guiding principles) to demonstrate the importance of the topic from their perspective. *Immigrant Neighbors among Us* is timely, because it demonstrates that Christians have not and cannot be indifferent to the situation of immigrants, or of the undocumented.

Each chapter challenges us to recognize that the Bible and most Christian traditions are very clear on the importance of caring for the migrant and the foreigner. Because they represent different theological traditions, there are clearly definable differences between the various authors and their arguments related to the sources of authority, to the level of participation in political action, to the role and power of the nation-state, and to the understanding of migrant integration into national culture and life. But all authors call Christians to work on behalf of justice for immigrants.

The authors clearly demonstrate that God cares about the undocumented and that we as Christians should care. But there are also differences as to what caring means and how one should care Christianly. These differences strengthen the book, because they invite readers to consider their own perspective and the biblical and theological basis for their position. Clearly, the authors want to influence the debate among Christians.

The book also comes from a distinctly Hispanic Christian perspective. All the authors are Latinos/as and have a history of service among immigrants, particularly undocumented Hispanics in the United States. This means that their work is not neutral. It clearly speaks from a perspective of commitment, of a desire to speak on behalf of those who are not allowed to have a voice in the immigration debates.

As an Anabaptist who is concerned about larger issues of justice, I realize that a very important issue that is not addressed in this book has to do with the causes of immigration. Today's migratory patterns have a history that was often created, or exploited, by the receiving countries. And the receiving countries often benefit from maintaining the status quo. Undoubtedly, it is not enough for Christians to seek justice for migrants. They must also confront the systems that benefit from undocumented migration and from limiting the rights of migrants. It would be very interesting for these authors to develop a second volume that presents biblical and theological responses to that issue.

Immigrant Neighbors among Us is a very important contribution from a distinctly Christian Hispanic perspective to a debate that is often polarized around political, social, and economic interests. The authors remind us that, because God cares, we are called to care. I want to thank the authors who remind us why we must care and how to do it. We must act, we must reflect, we must respond. Thank you for the challenge to do so.

Introduction

GIVEN THE NATIONAL AND international interest in immigration law and reform, it is surprising to note, with some exceptions, the relative dearth of theological works on immigration that offer sustained, ongoing, and explicit reflection from the perspective of Christian traditions.[1] Authors' levels of engagement with their own traditions' sources, though at times assumed in their writings, may not always be explicitly required by the scope or intent of their works on immigration issues. Official statements on immigration reform from denominations are available, but these documents are often too short or general to delve more deeply into the theological traditions that inspire them. This shortcoming is due in part to the occasional nature of such statements, written to address succinctly the immediate needs of immigrant neighbors in times of urgent crisis.[2] Rich in first-hand accounts of life and ministry among immigrants, pastoral reflections on immigration, like official church statements, are also written in critical times when church leaders sense the need to call their congregations to prayer, reflection, and action.[3]

We applaud and appreciate all of these contributions. At the same time, we believe that, as Christians encounter immigrant neighbors and think about immigration issues, they can benefit from a more explicit and

1. Notable book-length exceptions from Catholic scholars are Groody and Campese, eds., *A Promised Land*; and Kerwin and Gerschutz, eds., *And You Welcomed Me*; for a Lutheran contribution from a U.S. church body, see The Lutheran Church–Missouri Synod's Commission on Theology and Church Relations report *Immigrants Among Us*; see also chapters 4 through 7 in Padilla and Phan, eds., *Theology of Migration*.

2. For a list of official church statements on immigration, see Carroll R., *Christians at the Border*, 148–49.

3. For a recent pastoral contribution from a group of Catholic, Episcopal, Lutheran, and United Methodist bishops, see Adams et al., *Bishops on the Border*.

conscious attempt towards a critical and constructive engagement with the sources that inform their own church traditions. Yet theological and religious educators in university, seminary, or congregational settings, who are interested in such theological responses to immigration for courses or study groups, often have to gather resources from a variety of places in order to get a sense of what Christian traditions might contribute to the debate. Moreover, from a pedagogical point of view, it is often difficult to determine if a particular author speaks as an individual theologian, who may or may not be implicitly shaped by his or her tradition, or as an ecclesial theologian whose contribution is consciously drawn from such tradition and reflects an official stance. Making this distinction is difficult for instructors, who may be familiar with their own tradition's normative texts, events, or principles, but not with the guiding sources of other traditions.

The issue is not whether a theologian who engages the sources is better than one who works within more contemporary frameworks. Theologians may wear both hats in creative tension, depending on the audience and aims of their writings. Nor is it our aim to draw a false distinction between presumably more creative theologians, and those supposedly bound or enslaved to their ecclesial traditions. Everyone operates from within some canon (a tradition, narrowly or broadly defined), and every tradition requires not only a level of continuity through repetition but also ongoing, critical, and creative engagement with contemporary contexts. The authors in this book explicitly articulate and creatively engage their Christian traditions as they reflect on immigrant neighbors and immigration issues in a U.S. context. This volume, which brings together a number of representative voices, is relatively manageable in size and useful for classroom and study group use.

The voices in this book are Hispanic or Latina/o. The Hispanic population is most affected by national debates on immigration.[4] Given the proximity of our theologians to Hispanic immigrant neighbors, we feel a collective sense of calling, responsibility, and ownership concerning this issue. Besides demographics, the Hispanic contribution is a most critical voice in the scholarly conversation on immigration and related topics.[5] Our

---

4. The interest in Hispanic immigration is not surprising from a demographic perspective. For instance, most unauthorized immigrants in the U.S. are from Mexico (52% in 2012). Passel and Cohn, "Unauthorized Immigrant Totals," 9.

5. An illustrative number of contributions in biblical studies include Carroll R., *Christians at the Border*; Cuéllar, *Voices of Marginality*; and Ruiz, *Reading from the Edges*; historical and theological works include Badillo, *Latinos and the New Immigrant Church*;

writers embody a commitment to their Hispanic identity, churches, and communities, and strive to do theology with these neighbors in mind. In doing so, our authors look at their traditions' sources through Hispanic eyes, which includes particular attention to stories and experiences of exiles and aliens.[6] Our contributors seek to read their traditions' normative or guiding texts, histories, or experiences in light of the aspirations and struggles of vulnerable neighbors living on the move.

As representatives of our Christian traditions, we consciously ask what questions immigrant neighbors bring to our theological approaches, and how our traditions in turn shape what we say and do about immigration in the current situation. Our exploration may be described as a process of return to and (re-)appropriation of inspiring sources that in turn leads to a critical analysis of aspects of the tradition in need of rehabilitation or perhaps revision, constructive reflections on underdeveloped aspects, or applications or extensions of its familiar and guiding themes, categories, or narratives. Theologians from the same tradition may gather from the same sources a variety of responses for dealing with immigration issues in our day and age. Each voice in our work is representative or illustrative of his or her tradition and takes some of its key sources or principles seriously, without claiming to speak for all theologians in the same church family. Our reflections are thus invitations for others to engage in similar types of engagement with their respective ecclesial traditions and sources.

The number of theological traditions represented in this work is not exhaustive, but they are comprehensive enough to offer our readers a substantive taste of voices from a number of church families. Authors represent Roman Catholic, Lutheran, Reformed, Methodist/Wesleyan, Pentecostal, and Independent Evangelical traditions. In their reflections, the authors engage fields such as biblical studies, systematic and historical theology, ethics, and ministry. A brief summary of these contributions is now in order.

Arguing that the *magisterium* of the Roman Catholic Church reveals a rich yet often untapped resource of papal teaching on people on the move, Nanko-Fernández traces the major theological themes and developments on migrants and migration from Popes Pius XII to Francis. The author notes that the papal documents reveal a shift from the concern for the

---

Elizondo, *Galilean Journey*; and Machado, *Of Borders and Margins*. A significant number of Hispanic scholars have contributed articles in various anthologies such as Azaransky, ed., *Religion and Politics*; Isasi-Díaz and Segovia, eds., *Hispanic/Latino Theology*; and Fernandez and Segovia, eds., *A Dream Unfinished*.

6. See González, *Santa Biblia*, 91–102.

salvation of the souls of displaced Catholics to a respect for human dignity and solidarity for all displaced peoples—including families who have been separated through deportation. Moreover, the experience of migration functions as a biblical and theological metaphor for Catholic ecclesiology, namely, as a sign of the church's universal communion, her future hope in the heavenly city, and preferential option for migrants, refugees, and itinerant people around the world.

Proposing a rhetorical approach to immigration issues, Sánchez offers three thematic frameworks from Luther and the Lutheran tradition that can serve as entry points or guiding narratives for conversations on immigrants and immigration reform. Christ's identification with vulnerable strangers draws attention to immigrants, their struggles and hopes, and fits well with God's command to love the outsiders in the Old Testament as well as with Paul's teaching on evangelical hospitality in the New Testament. The Lutheran teaching on the two kingdoms or governments highlights God's twofold work in the world to justify humans before God (spiritual kingdom) and promote just relations among people in the civil realm (temporal kingdom). This model focuses on the Christian's twofold responsibility to foster the proclamation of the Gospel and works of mercy among immigrants, as well as the creation, enactment, and enforcement of fair immigration laws. Finally, the Lutheran teaching on vocation calls Christians to claim some neighbor and come to his or her defense. It challenges us to approach justice talk with a concrete neighbor in mind, including those immigrants and their children, who have over time become members of our families, churches, labor networks, and communities. Depending on the audience or conversation partners, some Lutheran frameworks may be more productive than others in engaging particular issues.

Firmly rooted in Calvin's life in exile as a resident alien and in the history of his work among persecuted refugees in Geneva, Rosario Rodríguez argues for a Reformed legacy of compassion towards and advocacy on behalf of immigrants today. The author persuasively weaves together Calvin's experience as a refugee, his theological portrayal of the Christian life as sojourn and exile in Book III of the *Institutes*, and his diaconal approach to the care of displaced persons in Geneva. Envisioning persecution and dispersion as a mark of the church, and the diaconate for the care of the poor as a divinely established church office, Calvinist theology is well positioned to foster a Christian response to immigration issues by prioritizing ministries of compassion and advocating for public policies that alleviate the suffering of powerless migrants who cannot speak for themselves.

Magallanes offers a Methodist/Wesleyan hermeneutic for assessing one's approach to immigration. Drawing on John Wesley's remarkable Aldersgate experience, which that pioneer described as a renewed assurance of Christ's salvation from the law of sin and death and a renewed commitment to pray for his enemies, the author proposes an approach to ethical issues that moves from merely dealing with others according to duty or law (at times, in a Pharisaical manner) to relating to them according to God's love in Christ. Such love is extended even to those one perceives as enemies. Ultimately, this is grounded in the divine purpose for Christians to strive towards reflecting the original image of a loving God in their lives—an image fully expressed in Christ's love for his enemies—as they make efforts to build relationships with immigrant neighbors today.

Taking as his starting point Christians' experiences of the Spirit's leading in their outreach to immigrant families through a church plant in Arizona, pastor and theologian Alfaro notes how Pentecostals have had to negotiate their traditionally passive approach to politics with a more proactive advocacy for large numbers of undocumented church members. Alfaro notes that Pentecostals make up for what they might lack in terms of formal theological statements by leveraging the theological and social implications of their grassroots practices and biblical commitments for reflection on immigration and the care of immigrants. He argues that a Pentecostal ethics begins with the praxis of Spirit-led hospitality, is nourished by the church's concern for the social dimension of evangelism (evident in ministries of healing and deliverance), and is willing to ask how the Spirit's power might manifest itself in the Christian's faith-based political activism on behalf of immigrant families.

Parting from an Evangelical commitment to the Scripture as a normative tradition in its own right, and utilizing the theme of exile as a hermeneutical lens in his approach to the ethics of the Old Testament, Carroll Rodas offers us a sketch of a biblical theology of immigration. The author argues that, while the Old Testament does not offer a blueprint for immigration law and reform, it nevertheless provides Christians with a moral compass to guide their reflection and action. Created in God's image, humans were designed as the Creator's special creatures to fill the earth, making the movements of people part of God's mysterious plan for the world. Similarly, the law of God was not only meant in antiquity as a blessing for

Israel but also for the surrounding nations. It included special provisions for the sojourner, which reflected foundational values that are relevant for the immigration debate today. The broad biblical material on migration can serve as windows that allow present-day readers—including immigrants—to remember God's special concern for sojourners and command to love them as the native in the land.

It is our hope that this work will encourage others to contribute to a broader conversation about perspectives on immigration law and reform. Our *U.S. Hispanic* focus invites other groups to speak from their ethnic and cultural situations to their own communities and to the broader church both in the U.S. and abroad. Our emphasis on Christian *traditions* invites other theological traditions unexplored in the present work to add their insights to the conversation. Such insights will facilitate the ongoing ecumenical task, which begins with our listening to, learning from, and collaborating with each other on issues of critical importance that affect all our communities. Our reflection from the perspective of Christian *theological* traditions raises broader questions about the methods and sources scholars in the field of religious studies or from various world religions use to speak about matters like immigration reform. These reflections can lead to productive interdisciplinary and interreligious dialogue on global migration.[7] Finally, our *immigration* focus invites further thought on the creative use of a theological or religious tradition's sources for exploring other societal issues such as poverty and marginality, women and gender issues, or the care of the environment.

A final word on the use of this book in teaching or study settings, whether in a church study group, university classroom, seminary or divinity school seminar, or Christian reading group. To spark thinking and dialogue, the end of each chapter offers questions for discussion. An appendix to the book includes a table that helps readers compare and contrast traditions. This table provides handy information on each theological tradition's key figures, major themes, biblical narratives, guiding sources, and other useful information. A second appendix contains a glossary of key terms. This volume closes with a composite bibliography drawn from the footnotes of all the chapters.

The editors would like to express a very heartfelt thanks to the authors for their insightful contributions to this book, Juan F. Martínez for providing the foreword, Danny Carroll Rodas's graduate assistant Brandon

7. For a recent contribution, see Padilla and Phan, eds., *Theology of Migration*.

Benziger for his tireless and detailed assistance in the preparation of the manuscript, and the editorial staff at Pickwick Publications for partnering with us in bringing this project to fruition. Many thanks to the leadership at Denver Seminary and at Concordia Seminary and its Center for Hispanic Studies, for supporting our scholarly efforts to reflect on the church's witness in the world in the midst of what is often a very heated national debate on immigration. Last but not least, we offer our thanksgiving to God for our spouses Joan and Tracy, our closest companions in this Christian pilgrimage we share together. Thank you for your unconditional love and support along the journey.

M. Daniel Carroll R.

and

Leopoldo A. Sánchez M.

Ash Wednesday 2015

Abbreviations

AHR	*American Historical Review*
BBR	*Bulletin for Biblical Research*
BJRL	*Bulletin of the John Rylands University Library of Manchester*
BZABR	Beiheifte zur Zeitschrift für Altorientalische und Biblische Rechtsgeschichte
CTJ	*Calvin Theological Journal*
FAT	Forschungen zum Alten Testament
JAAR	*Journal of the American Academy of Religion*
LCC	Library of Christian Classics
LW	*Luther's Works.* American ed. 55 vols. Edited by Jaroslav Pelikan and Helmut T. Lehman. Philadelphia: Fortress; St. Louis: Concordia, 1955–86.
PTMS	Princeton Theological Monograph Series
PTSSRTH	Princeton Theological Seminary Studies in Reformed Theology and History
R&T	*Religion and Theology*
SBL	Society of Biblical Literature
SemeiaST	Society of Biblical Literature Semeia Studies
Wesleyan Theol J	*Wesleyan Theological Journal*

—————— 1 ——————

A "Documented" Response[1]

Papal Teaching and People on the Move

Carmen M. Nanko-Fernández

IN 1965, THE LAST of the documents promulgated by the Second Vatican Council began with the stirring words, "The joys and the hopes, the griefs and the anxieties of the men [*sic*] of this age, especially those who are poor or in any way afflicted, these are the joys and hopes, the griefs and anxieties of the followers of Christ."[2] With this turn to the "signs of the times" and the obligation to scrutinize them critically in light of the Gospel, the Council situated the Roman Catholic Church firmly within the world. Today, set against the backdrop of unprecedented global migrations, Catholic communities across the globe and within the United States of America seek to understand themselves in terms of the world in the local church. Consider this example from Malaysia, a prominent migrant-receiving country. On a 2011 visit to St. John's Cathedral in Kuala Lumpur for Mass, Filipina theologian Gemma Tulud Cruz observed:

> . . . the diversity of the church goers was striking. Beside the local Catholics who were Indians and Chinese, there were Westerners as well as Asians and Africans from various countries . . . in that huge cathedral overflowing with people of various colors from various parts of the world, one gets a sense of the world church and a glimpse of what is probably the future of the church, that is

1. All Roman Catholic Church documents are listed under "Vatican Documents and Other Official Pronouncements" in the bibliography.

2. Vatican Council II, *Gaudium et Spes*, sec. 1.

an intercultural church brought about or, at the very least, reinforced by migration.[3]

Peoples in motion, many escaping poverty, lack of opportunity, civil strife, the aftermath of natural disasters, and/or oppression bring the world into the local church, across neighborhoods and barrios, in concrete ways. Marcelo M. Suárez-Orozco suggests that the phenomenon of globalization has created "homo sapiens mobilis." If all contemporary emigrants and immigrants were considered together they would comprise what he calls "Migration Nation," an entity third only to China and India in population.[4]

Concern by the Roman Catholic Church for people on the move is not only reserved for this most recent trend; it has been articulated across time in any number of venues especially from the highest levels of pastoral leadership.[5] This chapter will focus on the "documented" legacy of this Christian denomination and pay particular attention to the contributions of the pontificates of Pius XII (1939–1958) and Paul VI (1963–1978), followed by John Paul II (1978–2005), Benedict XVI (2005–2013), and Francis (2013–), three Bishops of Rome who themselves emigrate in order to fulfill the responsibilities of the office entrusted to them as "servants of the servants of God." It will conclude with an assessment—done *latinamente*—of key theological contributions and pastoral trajectories that this extensive body of documented teaching offers to ongoing public, ecumenical, and interreligious conversations on migration.

This overview is not from the grassroots but from the side of the magisterium, the teaching authority of the Roman Catholic Church. This survey is not exhaustive but focuses exclusively on select key papal teachings, a textual heritage that is evolving, rich, and documented. The use of the term "documented" with respect to the Church's teaching regarding people on the move is intentional. Catholics, among others, are often unaware of the substantial corpus of teaching on migration and itinerancy that has and continues to emanate from the Vatican across several centuries. Ignorance of these teachings makes it easier to dismiss the challenging positions taken more recently by local bishops and national bishops' conferences as meddling in political affairs or as reflections of so-called "liberal" agendas. Highlighting directives from the Vatican on migration matters is necessary, because there is an historical pattern of U.S. bishops

3. Cruz, "New Way of Being Christian," 95–96.

4. Suárez-Orozco, "Remittance Hole," 86.

5. For an historical overview see Baggio, "Migrant Ministry," 47–69.

failing to respond with pastoral urgency to matters of justice like slavery, racism, and desegregation.[6] Furthermore, these teachings and actions first emerged during pontificates most influenced by emigration from Europe toward *las Américas* in the late nineteenth and early twentieth centuries. U.S. Catholics tend to forget that there are many among us with ancestors, who arrived in these prior waves of immigration and were the objects of international pastoral concern. Finally, Catholicism is a denomination with a globally visible and central public figure that is both Bishop of Rome and head of state.[7] The Holy See functions as a sovereign entity with regard to matters of international relations, yet its diplomatic representatives and their activities are oriented toward the protection of human dignity and the common good rather than toward narrowly partisan political ends. In his 1963 radio message commemorating World Migration Day, Pope Paul VI reminded listeners of the tools at the Church's disposal to mitigate the trials of this global phenomenon: charitable assistance, diplomatic interventions, and the Church's teaching.[8]

6. Davis, *History of Black Catholics.* In this comprehensive history Davis points to such examples as the unwillingness of the U.S. bishops to denounce slavery, even though Pope Gregory XVI condemned the trade in 1839 in his apostolic letter *Supremo Apostolatus Fastigio.*

7. Bureau of European and Eurasian Affairs, "U.S. Relations with the Holy See."

8. Paul VI, "Radiomessaggio," para. 2: "L' Emigrazione—da un Paese all' altro, ovvero entro il territorio d' uno stesso Paese—costituisce oggi uno dei fenomeni più importanti e più gravi nella vita del mondo. La Chiesa, attenta e sollecita verso i problemi dell' umanità, non è stata indifferente davanti al problema dell' Emigrazione. . . . non ha tardato ad interessarsi con ogni mezzo a sua disposizione: quello dell' assistenza caritativa, quello degli interventi diplomatici, quello delle precisazioni dottrinali, per temperare i disagi ei disordini dell' emigrazione violenta, o forzata, o priva di guida e di aiuto." ("Immigration—from one country to another, or even within the territory of a single nation—is today one of the most important, and most serious phenomena in the life of the world. The Church, attentive and caring towards the problems of humanity, has not been indifferent to the problem of immigration. . . . It has not been slow to take an interest with every means at its disposal: that of charitable assistance, that of diplomatic interventions, that of doctrinal clarification, to temper the hardships and turmoil of violent or forced immigration, or [immigration] devoid of guidance and help." Trans. Gilberto Cavazos-González, O.F.M.)

Teaching Migration:
Before and *After* Vatican II

Concerns for people on the move and the rights and responsibilities of people in sending and receiving nations have been articulated in a trail of documentation that can be traced from Leo XIII through Francis. The teachings are communicated in a variety of formats, including but not limited to papal messages on the annual occasion of the World Day of Migrants and Refugees, apostolic constitutions, exhortations, letters, encyclicals, homilies, and documents from the Second Vatican Council.[9] These teachings were all formed in global contexts of several waves of human displacement and mobility.

Historically, the response of the Church to issues of people on the move has been framed with an impetus to pastoral action, attention to ecclesial juridical matters, and theological roots. Several key documents serve as classic examples of this framework: *Exsul Familia Nazarethana*, the 1952 encyclical of Pope Pius XII; *De Pastorali Migratorum Cura*, the 1969 Instruction from Sacred Congregation for Bishops, approved and authorized by Paul VI; and *Erga migrantes caritas Christi*, the 2004 instruction from the Pontifical Council for the Pastoral Care of Migrants and Itinerant People, approved and authorized by John Paul II.[10]

Pius XII (1939–1958) and *Exsul Familia Nazarethana* (1952)

The massive displacement of people during and in the aftermath of World War II insured that migration was a matter of concern in the papacy of Pius XII. In 1952 he issued *Exsul Familia Nazarethana* (EFN), named for the "émigré Holy Family of Nazareth, fleeing into Egypt," which he affirmed as "the archetype of every refugee family."[11] The first half of this Apostolic

---

9. Since 1915 the Church has annually recognized the World Day of Migrants and Refugees initiated by Benedict XV in response to the upheaval caused by World War I.

10. In 1912, Pius X established the *Officium de spirituali migratorum cura*, a special Office for the Pastoral Care of Migrants to coordinate the Church's efforts to improve conditions for migrants. Today it has evolved into the Pontifical Council for the Pastoral Care of Migrants and Itinerant People. For a brief history see "Pontifical Council."

11. Pius XII, *Exsul Familia Nazarethana*, #41 (see chs. 5 and 6). For original version in Latin see http://www.vatican.va/holy_father/pius_xii/apost_constitutions/documents/hf_p-xii_apc_19520801_exsul-familia_lt.html. The document contains an introduction and is divided into two sections: Title I, "The Church's Motherly Solicitude for Migrants";

Constitution contained a retrospective of what had been done in the past by the Church for the spiritual care of "pilgrims, aliens, exiles and migrants of every kind" (EFN, Title 1). Among the purposes for his wide-ranging account of examples of religious, moral, and social aid was the hope that the "universal and benevolent activity of the Church . . . might thus become better appreciated" (EFN, Title 1). Pius XII was motivated to trace this trajectory with specificity, in particular the contributions of his own pontificate, because he was disturbed by what he perceived as the Church being "unjustly assailed by her enemies and scorned and overlooked, even in the very field of charity where she was first to break ground and often the only to continue its cultivation" (EFN, Title 1).

The survey recapped a wealth of initiatives, especially those enacted by Pius XII himself and his immediate four papal predecessors, beginning with Leo XIII (1878–1903). He copiously cited endeavors focused on providing for the spiritual, sacramental, and even material needs of Catholics on the move. Among others, he included the founding of religious orders to serve and/or accompany migrants at various stages of their journey—points of departure, en route, and in resettlement; the establishment of seminaries to train clergy specifically for the apostolate to migrants; and the creation of national parishes to provide ministry "by priests of their own nationality or at least who speak their language" (EFN, Title 1). His inventory of actions on behalf of people on the move demonstrated an "eager co-operation of priests, members of religious communities and laymen"; however, as he observed, this "work has been carried out chiefly by priests who, in administering the Sacraments and preaching the Word of God, have labored zealously to strengthen the Faith of the Christians in the bond of charity" (EFN, Title 1).

The second half of this teaching spelled out norms for the spiritual care of migrants. In effect, this section updated the juridical responsibilities of varying levels of ministerial leadership from the special office in the Vatican to the local bishop to those missionaries, who worked specifically with migrants. Of particular note was the ongoing coordination of international efforts from the designated Vatican office (EFN, chs. 1 and 2); the affirmation of the responsibilities of the local receiving Church (EFN, ch. 4); the insistence on care that reflected sensitivity toward language and nationality

---

and Title II, "Norms for The Spiritual Care of Migrants." Title II is divided into six chapters where subsections are numbered. Citations referencing this document are provided in parentheses, in text, according to the abbreviated title, followed by chapter, and/or section number.

of origin; and a definition of immigrant that included those who migrate from colonies and the children of immigrants "even though they have acquired the rights of citizenship" (EFN, #40, nos. 1 and 2).

Theologically, Pius XII situated the Church's concern for people on the move in the Incarnation. The example of the Word-made-flesh and his family in flight were to serve "for all times and all places, the models and protectors of every migrant, alien and refugee of whatever kind who, whether compelled by fear of persecution or by want, is forced to leave his native land, his beloved parents and relatives, his close friends, and to seek a foreign soil" (EFN, Title 1). In this experience of "hardship and grief" the Son of God is also "the firstborn among many brethren, and precede them in it" (EFN, Title 1).

The obligation to care pastorally for migrating Catholics was also driven by a concern that migration and experiences in non-native lands left them vulnerable to a loss of faith and to ways of life that were not in conformity with moral law as interpreted by the Catholic Church. Therefore, the provision of spiritual care was necessary "to combat the evil work of those perverse men who, alas, associated with migrants under the pretext of bringing material aid, but with the intent of damaging their souls" (EFN, Title 1). Ultimately the salvation of souls was a primary theological motivation.

Paul VI (1963–1978) and *De Pastorali Migratorum Cura* (1969)

After the death of John XXIII, Pope Paul VI inherited the responsibility of carrying out the reforms of the Second Vatican Council. The Council's call for openness to the world and the global character of the Roman Catholic Church insured that there would be engagement on the questions of the day. In 1969 Pope Paul VI approved a revision of the norms propagated in *Exsul Familia Nazarethana*.[12] *De Pastorali Migratorum Cura* (DPMC) was released by the Sacred Congregation for Bishops.[13] It signified an update to the norms in light of the insights of the Second Vatican Council, convened

12. Paul VI, *Pastoralis Migratorum Cura*.

13. Sacred Congregation for Bishops, *De Pastorali Migratorum Cura* (*The Instruction on the Pastoral Care of Migrants*). The document was constructed simply with chapter one articulating fifteen points under the heading "General Principles" and chapters two though seven denoting the canonical norms. Citations referencing this document are provided in parentheses, in text, according to the abbreviated title, followed by chapter, and/or section number.

by his predecessor John XXIII (1958–1963), and responded to the changing reality of migration confronting the Church almost twenty years later.

The document began by recognizing the existence of new forms of migration. These shifts reflected rapid economic and technological progress as well as a growing global interdependence resulting from sociopolitical realities and advances in communication (DPMC, #1). The suffering, hazards, tensions, and conflicts inherent in migration were acknowledged, with specific mention of economic inequality and discriminations on the basis of gender, race, color, social condition, language, or place of origin (DPMC, #3). The document demonstrated an awareness of the array of differences across the spectrum of migrating peoples and included concern for those living outside of their respective homelands, "or their own ethnic community" (DPMC, #15). Practically speaking, the bishops remained acutely cognizant that, in the complex contexts of migrations, "the character of the service of souls to be offered by the Church should be this: that it be always suited to the needs of the immigrant people and that it remain adapted to them" (DPMC, #12).

Unlike *Exsul Familia Nazarethana*, the text did not recap historical precedents. Instead, it drew on the documents of Vatican II and the social teaching of Pope John XXIII to adapt pastoral praxis and expand theological grounds accordingly. A key addition was an explicit connection between concern for human rights and the pastoral care of souls. Pastoral care required ongoing consideration of these fundamental rights so that those who governed would protect them, and migrants would accept their duties as citizens and community members (DPMC, #5). Among the rights affirmed were the right to a homeland (DPMC, #6) and the right of individuals and families to emigrate and immigrate (DPMC, #7). From this perspective "the Church not only strives to offer the consolations of religion to all emigrants, but also zealously struggles for the sanction and preservation of the rights of the human person and of the foundations of his spiritual life" (DPMC, #4). The practical responsibility for this protection of human rights fell to the laity (DPMC, #57). National bishops conferences were instructed to promote dialogue internationally and nationally with those associations, individuals, organizations, and government agencies necessary to better "foster the rights of people who migrate, even in social matters" (DPMC, #23, sec. 6).

Sensitivity for the culture and language of migrants was reaffirmed in the directives for pastoral care and reframed in terms of "the right of keeping one's native tongue and spiritual heritage" (DPMC, #11). The teaching recognized the interrelationship between language, worldview, and spiritual life as a value that would endure and should "be prized highly everywhere" (DPMC, #11). The commitment of the Church to provide ministry in the languages of immigrants was reiterated over twenty times in the chapters addressing norms. The strongest admonition appeared in the section addressed to local bishops in conjunction with the celebration of liturgy: "the ordinaries of the place are not to refuse to admit the use of the immigrants' own language in the Sacred Liturgy, no matter what country they come from" (DPMC, #32).

Like *Exsul Familia Nazarethana*, the presentation of norms was ordered hierarchically. In other words, they began with the responsibilities of those in ministerial leadership; however, a significant addition was the inclusion of a chapter related specifically to the participation of the laity (DPMC, ch. 7). Among the responsibilities delineated for the laity were the protections of the civil rights of immigrants, especially as they pertained to the preservation of the family (DPMC, #57). The primary duties of the laity rested in the temporal sphere for which their skills and influence were considered best suited. Their witness as active participants in the life of faith was recognized for its evangelizing potential.

> Let them participate actively in the liturgy, so that divine worship may be attractive to souls. Let them communicate the Word of God to the various ethnic groups when the occasion offers and in the manner proper to lay people. What is even more important, when distance or scattered location or lack of clergy of their own people or of the place deprive immigrant people of religious care, let the laity zealously seek them out, receive them hospitably, comfort them, and introduce them to the local church. (DPMC, #58)

The intentional focus on rights suggests a shift to a theological anthropology that has an ethical dimension. In other words, respect for human dignity emerged as foundational in shaping responses to migration. Mutuality was called for in relationships between those who left their native lands and those nations and communities who received these newcomers. Immigrants were to be welcomed as kin "endowed with human dignity and builders of a new and broader human community" (DPMC, #57). Therefore, rights were to be protected in acquiescence to the demands of truth, love and justice, and in preservation of the unity of the human family. The work of the Holy Spirit was perceived in impulses toward the unification of global humanity arising from the movements of peoples (DPMC, #2). The roots of the principle of solidarity in Catholic Social Teaching were evident here in calls for mutuality in respect, understanding, and cooperation among peoples and social entities.

The interreligious and ecumenical implications of migration generated pastoral concern. The document indicated an appreciation for the religious pluralism that marked the new reality of migration, especially as it was experienced in quotidian encounters (DPMC, #13). Migrations presented opportunities for cooperative ventures to promote Christian unity, and for Christians to bear living witness to those who were either of other religious traditions or non-believers (DPMC, #13). This commitment to all people on the move was enshrined in the norms as well. Local bishops were directed to "benignly and willingly assist other Christians who do not enjoy full communion with the Catholic Church and who lack ministers of their church or community; nor are they to deny assistance to non-Christian people if they come" (DPMC, #30, sec. 2).

Migrant Pope: John Paul II (1978–2005)

The pontificate of John Paul II, the first non-Italian pope since 1523, was marked by a sense of motion. The election of Karol Wojtyla as Bishop of Rome made him a migrant worker, who, like countless others, would have opportunities to visit his homeland but would be buried in the place of his sojourn. A native of Poland, he referenced this call from a "distant land" in his first message as Pope,[14] and during his tenure he earned distinction by visiting 129 countries in 104 trips over six continents between 1979 and 2004.[15] The length of his term in office, the second longest in history, allowed him to produce a significant body of teaching and preaching on migration.[16] Perhaps one of the most overlooked references occurred in his forceful reiteration of a "number of crimes and attacks against human life" identified in the Vatican II constitution *Gaudium et Spes*. In his encyclical

14. John Paul II, "Primo Saluto," para. 1: "Lo hanno chiamato da un paese lontano . . . lontano, ma sempre così vicino per la comunione nella fedeli e nella tradizione cristiana" ("First Greeting," para. 1: "They [the Cardinals] have called him from a distant country . . . far away but close always by communion in faith and Christian tradition.").

15. For the complete list of his travels, with links to additional photos and texts, see "John Paul II: Travels," http://www.vatican.va/holy_father/john_paul_ii/travels/.

16. For links to these messages see "John Paul II: Messages, World Migration Days," http://www.vatican.va/holy_father/john_paul_ii/messages/migration/index.htm.

Evangelium Vitae, John Paul affirmed "that condemnation in the name of the whole Church, certain that I am interpreting the genuine sentiment of every upright conscience."[17] Included on the list of acts that opposed life and insulted human dignity (along with genocide, abortion, torture, human trafficking) was deportation. Perhaps this should come as no surprise, considering Wojtyla's formative young adulthood was spent surviving in Nazi-occupied Poland.

In the last year of his pontificate John Paul II approved and authorized the publication of *Erga migrantes caritas Christi* (EMCC) by the Pontifical Council for the Pastoral Care of Migrants and Itinerant People.[18] It was released thirty-five years after *De Pastorali Migratorum Cura* and in many ways reflected the theological and pastoral approaches advanced in his pontificate. Like its two predecessors, this document consisted of an examination of the state of migration in the context of its times followed by a distinct section updating canonical norms pertinent to the pastoral care of people on the move. It remained consistent with the past in recognizing the right to migrate and in affirming that conditions at home should be such that one should not have to emigrate in order to provide for family and sustain an economically, socially, and politically stable life (EMCC, #29). Like *Exsul Familia Nazarethana,* it reviewed historical antecedents in magisterial teaching, juridical regulations, and pastoral responses from the highest levels of Church leadership (EMCC, #19–33). Primarily, the instruction sought to "respond to the new spiritual and pastoral needs of migrants." Another dimension rose to the forefront, an intention "to make migration more and more an instrument of dialogue and proclamation of the Christian message" (EMCC, #3).

Toward these purposes, the instruction further developed several earlier threads. It explicitly advocated for the human rights of migrants and articulated a growing concern for the exploitation of migrant labor and the increase of women and families on the move. The instruction reflected significant development in an understanding of solidarity. It called for a "culture of solidarity" (EMCC, #9) that included welcome and was reflected in the church, personal attitudes, communal responses, national policies, and even in relationships among nations. Solidarity was considered to be a

17. John Paul II, *Evangelium Vitae,* sec. 3.

18. Pontifical Council for the Pastoral Care of Migrants and Itinerant People, *Erga migrantes caritas Christi.* Citations referencing this document are provided in parentheses, in text, according to the abbreviated title, followed by section number.

value, a behavior (EMCC, #30), and a commitment, which manifests "not only a support . . . but also a witness to values that can enkindle hope in sad situations" (EMCC, #83). The instruction urged ongoing attention to the ecumenical and interreligious implications of this global phenomenon, encouraging Christians to be educated so that "the faithful may discover the *semina Verbi* (seeds of the Word) found in different cultures and religions" (EMCC, #96).

Further developments were evident in areas relating to the responsibilities of the laity and in practical considerations of inculturation. In terms of the laity, their responsibilities were delineated first, not last in the juridical section (EMCC, ch. 1, arts. 2–3), a reversing of the hierarchical order present in the past documents. Laity was instructed to "welcome migrants as brothers and sisters" and to insure the protection of their civil rights, including the preservation of the unity of their families (EMCC, art. 2). While past documents focused on the laity primarily in the temporal sphere (EMCC, #87), here the lay faithful were more often addressed as evangelizers, who give witness through their lives and are also called increasingly to engage in the "typical tasks of *diakonia*," especially where clergy shortage impacts the ability of the church to minister with migrants (EMCC, #86–88, art. 2.2, art. 3.4). The migrant laity was called "to esteem the cultural patrimony of the nation that welcomes them, to contribute to its common good and to spread the faith especially by the example of Christian life" (EMCC, art. 3.1). At the same time, the local church was expected to insure that migrant laity, especially in regions where they are numerous, have access to participate in decision-making diocesan and parochial structures (EMCC, art. 3.2).

The document affirmed the ongoing commitment of the Church for providing pastoral care that is accommodating to migrants and mindful of "their legitimate diversity and of their spiritual and cultural patrimony" (EMCC, #9). Consistent with past teaching, this commitment entailed the provision of culturally and linguistically appropriate care and opportunities to practice the faith. These pastoral obligations must be enacted at the local territorial level of the diocese and the parish, and across sending and receiving churches.

As evident through his travels and numerous encyclicals and messages, the relationship between faith and culture in pluralistic contexts was of particular interest to John Paul II. For the Church, the magnitude of contemporary migration introduced unprecedented cultural and religious pluralism experienced in part because of advances in technology and media (EMCC, #35). Migrations created possibilities for multiple interactions among "cultural and religious backgrounds, traditionally different and foreign to one another"; these situations required skills in listening and dialogue (EMCC, #35–36). The ecclesial response throughout the pontificate of John Paul II included a construal of inculturation, whereby the task of the magisterium was to direct and discern the validity of varying cultural interpretations of the Gospel (EMCC, #36). Inculturation, which assumed postures of respect and openness to dialogue, was at the heart of evangelization.

Of the three documents that include juridical norms, *Erga migrantes caritas Christi* is the most theologically oriented. First, it is the only one of the three to use scripture in a thematic manner. Through the eyes of faith, migration is considered within the biblical tapestry of salvation history "as a sign of the times and of the presence of God in history and in the community of peoples, directed to universal communion" (EMCC, #13–18, Presentation). Second, it finds eschatological significance in migration (EMCC, #17). Again through faith, migrations serve as a reminder of how "we are all pilgrims on our way towards our true homeland" (EMCC, #101). In their journeys migrants offer "a constant stimulus to that hope which points to a future beyond this present world, inspiring the transformation of the world in love and eschatological victory" (EMCC, #18). Third, protection of migrants is grounded in a theological anthropology that holds human dignity as a foundational principle. The ethical responsibility to protect life, especially at its most vulnerable, is accomplished by insuring a basic quality of life through the preservation of human rights, thus manifesting respect for God-given human dignity. Finally, in migration and in the diversity it inevitably engenders and represents, the document finds ecclesiological and missiological significance. Integral to the life of the Church, migration is perceived in terms of its ability to reflect universality, impact future expansion, and promote internal communion (EMCC, #97).

> Migration thus offers the *Church* an historic opportunity to prove its four characteristic marks: the Church is *one* because in a certain sense it also expresses the unity of the whole human family; it is *holy* also to make all people holy and that God's name may be sanctified in them; it is *catholic* furthermore in its openness to diversity that is to be harmonised; and it is likewise *apostolic* because it is also committed to evangelise the whole human person and all people. (EMCC, #97)

Immigrant Pope: Benedict XVI (2005–2013)

Josef Ratzinger immigrated to Vatican City from Germany in 1981 to head the Congregation for the Doctrine of the Faith. Like John Paul II, he lived through the trauma of World War II and its aftermath.[19] Ratzinger, taking the name Benedict XVI, was elected Bishop of Rome in April 2005 at age 78 and resigned his office in February 2013. He continues to live in Vatican City as the first Bishop of Rome Emeritus. During his eight-year pontificate Benedict XVI made 24 trips outside of Italy and visited 26 countries; over half were European nations, with four trips to the Iberian Peninsula.

Benedict dealt with migration primarily through the annual World Migration Day messages.[20] Recurrent themes included particular concerns for migrant youth and children (2008, 2010), families (2007), international students, and human trafficking. In his 2011 message, one line in particular captured the attention of those who misinterpreted it as a modification in Church support for immigrants. Benedict wrote: "At the same time, States have the right to regulate migration flows and to defend their own frontiers, always guaranteeing the respect due to the dignity of each and every human person. Immigrants, moreover, have the duty to integrate into the host Country, respecting its laws and its national identity."[21] In his 2013 message, Benedict repeated the right of states to regulate migration with policies, mindful of the common good which must always take care to safeguard human dignity.[22] Like Pius XII and John Paul II, Benedict did not treat this need to exercise control over sovereign borders as an absolute right.[23]

19. Ratzinger, *Milestones*, 12–40.

20. For links to the texts of these messages see Benedict XVI, "World Migration Days: Messages," http://www.vatican.va/holy_father/benedict_xvi/messages/migration/index_en.htm.

21. Benedict XVI, "One Human Family," para. 5.

22. Benedict XVI, "Migrations."

23. On Christmas Eve 1948 Pius XII wrote to the U.S. Bishops, "the sovereignty of the State, although it must be respected, cannot be exaggerated to the point that access to this land is, for inadequate or unjustified reasons, denied to needy and decent people from other nations, provided of course, that the public wealth, considered very carefully, does not forbid this" (cited in *Exsul Familia Nazarethana*). In early 2001 John Paul II wrote, "Certainly, the exercise of such a right is to be regulated, because practicing it indiscriminately may do harm and be detrimental to the common good of the community that receives the migrant. Before the manifold interests that are interwoven side by side with the laws of the individual countries, it is necessary to have international norms that are capable of regulating everyone's rights, so as to prevent unilateral decisions that are harmful to the weakest." John Paul II, "Pastoral Care of Migrants," sec. 3.

This concern was qualified by a desire to protect, from exploitation and trafficking, those migrants made vulnerable by "irregular migration." His understanding of "an orderly migration policy" opposed efforts that "end up in a hermetic sealing of borders, more severe sanctions against irregular migrants and the adoption of measures meant to discourage new entries."[24] He called for legislative actions, international cooperation, an expansion of humanitarian protections beyond political asylum, and "for a patient and persevering effort to form minds and consciences."[25]

References by Benedict to migration occur briefly in his social encyclical *Caritas in Veritate,* and in homilies and remarks during his only visit to the United States of America. In his social encyclical, Benedict acknowledged the challenges faced by all in managing migration as a global phenomenon of epic proportions. He demonstrated particular concern for workers, pointing to their economic contributions to the host country through their labor and to their homeland through remittances. Benedict urged collaborative international efforts to protect migrants and their families as well as host nations.[26]

In 2008 Benedict began his visit to the U.S. by fielding questions from reporters on his inbound flight. The second question dealt with immigration and the Hispanic presence in the U.S. In his reply, Benedict distinguished between long and short-term solutions. Consistent with his predecessors, he pressed for international cooperation to insure the type of "social development that makes it possible to offer citizens work and a future in their homeland."[27] His short-term measures addressed the protection of families "to prevent precariousness and every kind of violence, and to help so that they may really have a dignified life wherever they may be."[28] He did not address the question of the growing Hispanic presence directly; however, he began his response with "I cannot speak Spanish but *mis saludos y mi bendición para todos los hispánicos*" ("my greetings and my blessing for all Hispanics").[29] Throughout his trip, at the outdoor public Masses and at certain venues in Washington DC and New York, he intentionally included

24. Benedict XVI, "Migrations," para. 7.
25. Ibid.
26. Benedict XVI, *Caritas in Veritate.*
27. Benedict XVI, "Interview of the Holy Father," para. 8.
28. Ibid.
29. Ibid.

remarks in Spanish.[30] In his homily at Nationals Stadium in Washington DC he attributed the growth in the U.S. Catholic Church to the welcome of immigrants and to "*la vitalidad del testimonio de fe de los fieles de lengua española*" ("the vitality of the testimony of faith of the Spanish-speaking faithful"). He pointed to the evangelizing potential of the Latino and Latina faithful, who, in union with Christ and each other, would be a source for peace and reconciliation in a world too often marked by division and confrontation.[31]

Re-asporic Pope: Francis (2013–)

In so many ways the papacy of Francis, the first pope from Latin America—a Spanish-speaking son of Italian immigrants—reflects contemporary realities of global motion, interconnectivity, and hybridity. It should be no surprise then that his first papal visit outside of Rome was to Lampedusa, a small island off the Sicilian coast that serves as entry point to the European Union for tens of thousands of migrants and refugees.[32] Driven by the haunting image of the tragic death of immigrants at sea, "a painful thorn in my heart," he came "to pray and to offer a sign of my closeness, but also to challenge our consciences."[33] Altar, cross, and pulpit—fashioned from the remnants of boats that carried migrants and refugees—bore witness to the "globalization of indifference" that "makes us all 'unnamed', responsible, yet nameless and faceless."[34]

The return of Jorge Bergoglio to Italy, the home of his diasporic parents, represents a reaspora of sorts for both Europe as well as the Roman Catholic Church. The term "reaspora" was coined initially as a reference

30. Benedict XVI included remarks in Spanish at the following events: "Homily" (April 17, 2008); "Meeting With Young People and Seminarians"; "Homily" (April 20, 2008).

31. Benedict XVI, "Homily" (April 17, 2008): "La Iglesia en los Estados Unidos, acogiendo en su seno a tantos de sus hijos emigrantes, ha ido creciendo gracias también a la vitalidad del testimonio de fe de los fieles de lengua española. Por eso, el Señor les llama a seguir contribuyendo al futuro de la Iglesia en este País y a la difusión del Evangelio. Sólo si están unidos a Cristo y entre ustedes, su testimonio evangelizador será creíble y florecerá en copiosos frutos de paz y reconciliación en medio de un mundo muchas veces marcado por divisiones y enfrentamientos."

32. Francis, "Visit to Lampedusa," includes schedule, homily, video, and photo gallery.

33. Francis, "Homily," para. 1.

34. Ibid., para. 7.

to "members of the diaspora who are returning and getting into business, the marketplace and service in their home countries."[35] First used among diasporic Africans, primarily in social media, it marks a reversal of the so-called "brain drain."[36] It signals a counter-migration, often overlooked in religious and theological scholarship, a return home by immigrants and/ or their descendants. Culture studies scholar, Juan Flores, playing with language and return in Puerto Rican contexts, invented the term "Re-aspori-can." He studies "the reverse flow or 'counterstream' resulting from massive circular and return migration and the ongoing remittance of cultural values and practices through friends, relatives and the media."[37] For Flores, these Re-asporicans signify tension and promise, challenges and changes forged "in this highly charged collision of distinct but intertwined experiences" generated in the flows and counter-flows of diaspora.[38]

What does a re-asporic Pope, from the "ends of the earth,"[39] add to the already rich heritage of Catholic teaching on migrations? Francis moves into the center of the Vatican an embodied commitment to the preferential option for the poor and vulnerable. He also conveys a familiarity with Latin American theologies of liberation. These are not abstractions. Instead, they are integral to the lived daily experiences Jorge Bergoglio brings to the office of Bishop of Rome. He effectively communicates this commitment in his papacy through symbolic actions, brief homilies, audiences, and even tweets.[40]

From the beginning of his papacy, through words and actions, Francis has identified migration-related issues among his priorities. In his Apostolic Exhortation, *Evangelii Gaudium* (EG), he acknowledges migrants pose "a particular challenge for me, since I am the pastor of a Church without frontiers, a Church which considers herself mother to all" (EG, #210).[41]

---

35. Kaigwa, "D8A's 8 Lessons."

36. TMS Ruge, "Message to Davos."

37. Flores, *Diaspora Strikes Back*, 4.

38. Ibid.

39. Francis, "Apostolic Blessing 'Urbi et Orbi,'" para. 1: "You know that it was the duty of the Conclave to give Rome a Bishop. It seems that my brother Cardinals have gone to the ends of the earth to get one... but here we are..."

40. Pope Francis, https://twitter.com/Pontifex (July 8, 2013): "We pray for a heart which will embrace immigrants. God will judge us upon how we have treated the most needy."

41. Francis, *Evangelii Gaudium*. Citations referencing this document are provided in parentheses, in text, according to the abbreviated title, followed by section number.

This responsibility serves as impetus for his encouragement to all nations to assume a posture of "generous openness," which has the capacity "of creating new forms of cultural synthesis" rather than "fearing the loss of local identity" (EG, #210). He notes, "How beautiful are those cities which overcome paralysing mistrust, integrate those who are different and make this very integration a new factor of development!" (EG, #210).

In *Evangelii Gaudium*, Francis treats migration within the section addressing the option for the poor and concern for the vulnerable. He presents migration as part of "new forms of poverty and vulnerability, in which we are called to recognize the suffering Christ" (EG, #210). He then draws particular attention to a disturbing dimension of mobility—human trafficking—and charges that all are complicit in networks of crime that involve killing of our brothers and sisters in "clandestine warehouses, in rings of prostitution, in children used for begging, in exploiting undocumented labour" (EG, #211). He grounds this challenge to the many people with "blood on their hands as a result of their comfortable and silent complicity" in the haunting question to Cain "where is your brother?" (EG, #211).

Assessing a Documented History— *Latinamente*

Latina/Hispanic theologies tend to begin with the grassroots and look to popular practice and movements in exploring slices of daily lived experience. In this case, the move to investigate migration through authoritative teachings from the side of ecclesial leadership may appear counterintuitive *latinamente*. In reality, it is not. The point of departure for this exposition is the daily lived experience of ignorance among too many Catholics in the pews and in positions of secular power, who remain unaware of the depth, breadth, and authority of their own denomination's historical stance on migration. To assess this vast body of teaching is a massive task beyond the scope of this survey; however, from a Latina theological perspective three threads merit further commentary.

Preferential Options

The preferential option for the poor entered papal vocabulary in 1980 during the visit of John Paul II to Brazil. The option was first articulated in this manner by the conference of Latin American bishops (CELAM) and developed by Latin American liberation theologians in the late 1970s. Over the past three decades it has become a recognized principle of Catholic social teaching.[42] In effect, the option affirms that the needs of the poor and vulnerable have a moral claim on the community and as such serve as criteria for consideration of the common good. Policies, actions, and practices are to be evaluated in terms of their impact on the least and most vulnerable. Migrants, refugees, and itinerant peoples are included among the poor and vulnerable.

Clearly, the teachings of the magisterium make an intentional option for people on the move, even before the language of preferential option entered the Church's lexicon. In papal teaching from Leo XIII through Francis, migrants are considered individually and collectively as people whose condition places them in need of protection throughout their journey and sojourn. Furthermore, this concern has been articulated in calls for the protection of rights; the provision of opportunities for participation in the life of Church, society, and nation; and ministry that is sensitive to cultural and linguistic particularities and expressions of the faith. Unfortunately, in the current climate of polarization, created by a vocal few who feed xenophobia, the Church's option for migrants is considered to be a recent phenomenon. Few recall that in papal teaching, historically, only one national community, considered a "problem" especially in the United States and Australia, was singled out for ongoing special consideration.

In his 1888 encyclical to the U.S. Bishops on Italian emigration Leo XIII responded to his compatriots' plight, citing his obligation "to prepare healthy pastures, and by every possible exertion to advance their salvation and their good" in part because "the love for men who spring from the same race as ourselves makes Us more zealous for their benefit . . . ."[43] This papal concern for Italian migrants in particular continued in his successors, and was evident in Pius XII's *Exsul Familia Nazarethana* (1952). In the section delineating norms for the spiritual care of migrants, Italians are the only nationality singled out with special attention and an acknowledgement by Pius XII of this longstanding papal practice. He writes,

> Since migration has been more common among Italians than other peoples, the Holy See has been especially active in caring for Italian migrants. We, by this Apostolic Letter, confirm those special regulations drawn up by our predecessors with regard to

42. See Nanko-Fernández, *Theologizing en Espanglish*, 120–52.
43. Leo XIII, *Quam Aerumnosa*, sec. 3.

Italians emigrating to foreign countries. . . . We take this opportunity to urge these local Ordinaries earnestly to fulfill our wishes.[44]

This historical reality complicates the current immigration debate and challenges positions that seek to dismiss the Church's advocacy on behalf of migrants. It also raises questions for descendants of immigrants: What happens when people forget the options made for them and their ancestors? What happens when they forget that their parents or grandparents were once considered "the problem"?

Familia

Across magisterial teaching, migration has been regarded as a family matter, with particular attention to the vulnerability of women and children, especially with regards to human trafficking and for maintaining the unity of families. In the United States, the Catholic bishops have supported comprehensive and just immigration reform, which explicitly includes attentiveness to families and a reduction of the waiting period that currently hampers reunification. At the same time, the bishops have opposed the inclusion of the Uniting American Families Act (UAFA) in legislation aimed at immigration reform, perceiving it as an obstacle to their public support. According to the U.S. bishops, "This legislation would erode the unique meaning of marriage by allocating spousal immigration benefits to persons in same-sex relationships. The inclusion of this provision would unnecessarily introduce controversy into an already divisive debate."[45]

How is this stance to be reconciled with the 1996 World Migrant Day message of John Paul II: "It is necessary to avoid recourse to the use of administrative regulations, meant to restrict the criterion of family membership which result in unjustifiably forcing into an illegal situation people whose right to live with their family cannot be denied by any law"?[46] Granted, the legalization of same-sex marriage may not have entered into his deliberations, but, whether intended or not, there is a magisterial caution here about the risks migrants face when the definition of family is too narrowly constructed.

---

44. Pius XII, *Exsul Familia Nazarethana*, #41 (see chs. 5 and 6).

45. Gomez, "Testimony," 11.

46. John Paul II, "Undocumented Migrants," sec. 4.

Convivencia

The expectation that migrants are to have access to care and expressions of faith that are linguistically and culturally respectful remains consistent. Left underexplored is how interaction with varied worldviews, religious beliefs, and diverse expressions of the Catholic faith might enrich the life and practices of the church and society in host lands, and influence magisterial teaching. Any cultivation of dialogue and mutual respect cannot ignore the dynamics of power and privilege that are at play in the reconfiguration of space and communities.

The phenomenon of migration brings human differences of all kinds into our churches, our neighborhoods, and within our respective national borders. From the perspective of faith, as articulated in magisterial teaching, this new diverse reality is rich in theological significance. First, for Catholics, migrations signify the universality of the Church, a communion not restricted by ethnicity, race, culture, or social class. At the same time, people on the move point to the universal kinship of the human family which necessarily requires, at the very least, tolerance, respect for identity, and an appreciation for religious and cultural pluralism. In order to carefully navigate the tensions and nurture constructive relationships across differences, the teachings call for a culture of solidarity.

Ultimately, global migrations call nations and neighborhoods, faith communities and families to reconsider how to achieve a just, fruitful, and peaceful *convivencia*, literally a "living together." For Catholics these deliberations include an extensive "documented" legacy that continues to evolve.

Discussion Questions

1. Pope Pius XII referred to the "émigré Holy Family of Nazareth, fleeing into Egypt" as "the archetype of every refugee family." What difference does it make for you, your faith, or your approach to immigrant neighbors to think of Jesus and his family as persecuted refugees?

2. *The Instruction on the Pastoral Care of Migrants* notes that the church's pastoral care of immigrant people must go hand in hand with a serious concern for their human dignity and rights. How do you understand the relationship between the spiritual care of people and advocacy

for their rights? How might that relationship play out in your way of thinking about interacting with immigrants?

3. In the Instruction *Erga migrantes caritas Christi* laity are instructed to be evangelizers, who "welcome migrants as brothers and sisters," and migrant laity are called "to esteem the cultural patrimony of the nation that welcomes them, to contribute to its common good and to spread the faith especially by the example of Christian life." In what way(s) do (can) laity in your church welcome migrants? How do (can) migrants in your community contribute to the common good of the nation and the work of the church?

4. Pope Benedict XVI acknowledges that "States have the right to regulate migration flows and to defend their own frontiers," but he also speaks against "a hermetic sealing of borders, more severe sanctions against irregular immigrants and the adoption of measures meant to discourage new entries." How might these two insights or principles be useful for thinking through proposals for immigration law and reform?

5. In the final section of the essay, the author highlights three factors that shape a Roman Catholic contribution to immigration issues from a Latina/o perspective. These factors are the preferential option for vulnerable migrants, the protection of the family (especially women and children), and the appreciation for migrations as a sign of the universality of the church. Which one of these factors is most critical for you as you think about immigrants and immigration? Are there other issues that also need careful consideration?

———— 2 ————

Who Is My Neighbor?
Immigration through Lutheran Eyes

Leopoldo A. Sánchez M.

Introduction

THE HEIRS OF THE Reformation inspired by Martin Luther have access to
theological sources that are promising for engaging various aspects of the
immigration debate today. In this essay, I argue that an ethic inspired by the
Lutheran theological tradition allows for a spectrum of positions on immigration law and reform, which are arrived at on the basis of the competing
claims of various advocates on behalf of different neighbors. These claims
are in turn informed by different themes found in Lutheran theology to
approach ethical issues, namely, Christ's self-identification with vulnerable
neighbors, God's work in the world through the two kingdoms or governments, and the Christian's calling or vocation in society. I will focus mainly
on selections from Luther's writings that deal with ethics or life together in
relationship to neighbors, asking what these sources have to offer today to
a discussion on immigration.

Each Lutheran source offers a unique entry point into the immigration debate by focusing on a particular thematic center. The first framework
centers on the vulnerable neighbor as the main narrative, highlighting
how Luther's Christological teaching allows us to speak of the church's call
to love needy pilgrims like pregnant Mary in the city of Bethlehem. The
second framework focuses on God's world as the dominant theme in the
immigration debate, stressing how God preserves creation in a twofold

manner, namely, through the temporal realm by means of law and for the sake of peace in society, and through the spiritual realm by means of the Gospel for the sake of bringing people into communion with God through faith in Christ. This teaching on the two kingdoms or governments raises questions related to the Christian's responsibilities towards neighbors in both realms of divine activity, seeking both justice before one another (temporal government) and justification before God through Christ (spiritual government). The third framework centers on the Christian's vocation in church and society as the main narrative for shaping a discussion on immigration, focusing on how our vocational location shapes concretely which neighbors we choose to defend and which issues we choose to advocate for in the debate.

Welcoming Vulnerable Strangers: Christ's Self-Identification with the Needy

A growing number of U.S. Hispanic communities celebrate Christmas by recalling the arduous journey of Joseph and his pregnant wife Mary from Nazareth in Galilee to Bethlehem in Judea (Luke 2:1–7). Caesar Augustus had ordered a census that required all subjects living under Roman rule to register in their town of origin. Joseph migrated with Mary, who was with child, to Bethlehem, the city of his ancestor David. Sometime after arriving to the city, Mary gave birth to Jesus, "her firstborn son and wrapped him in swaddling cloths and laid him in a manger, because there was no place for them in the inn" (v. 7).[1]

In the Hispanic Christian imagination, a religious tradition called *Las Posadas* began to develop around the Holy Family's search for a place—an inn, a *posada*—for Mary and baby Jesus to rest. To retell the biblical story, pilgrims (*peregrinos*) journey with Joseph, Mary, and baby Jesus, knocking on neighborhood doors, in search for *posada*, only to be turned away repeatedly by untrusting, mean, or apathetic innkeepers (*posaderos*). When all hope is lost, at the very last house, Jesus, his family, and pilgrims who accompany and follow them, are warmly welcomed by a gracious innkeeper whose eyes are opened to see the gift of God who has visited him. Finally, a celebration, a great *fiesta*, breaks out as pilgrims rejoice at the visitation of Jesus Christ, the Savior, in their homes and hearts.

---

1. All biblical citations are taken from the English Standard Version.

Is it you, Joseph?
Is your wife Mary?
Enter, pilgrims,
I had not met you.[2]

Enter holy pilgrims, pilgrims,
accept this corner,
not of this poor abode,
but of my soul.[3]

Various Christian themes coalesce in the liturgical rhythm of *Las Posadas*, as pilgrims and innkeepers alike participate in the retelling of the biblical story. It is a story of hostility towards strangers, the babe's vulnerability, and unbelief in him. It is also a story of hospitality, charity, and faith. Immigrant pilgrims in the U.S. readily identify with Jesus and his family, with their experiences of marginality and rejection, but also love and hospitality towards strangers.

While the practice of *posadas* has been traced back to late sixteenth century Mexico as a catechetical means to teach Amerindian converts about Jesus' birth, *posada* themes are inspired in the fifteenth century Spanish *villancico* (carol) medieval tradition.[4] Around the times these traditions develop in the Old and New Worlds, the air of church reform was spreading across Europe, particularly in the land of an Augustinian monk called Martin Luther. On 31 October 1517, Luther nailed his now famous Ninety-Five Theses to the door of All Saints' Church in Wittenberg, an occasion that has now become the most prominent symbol of the Protestant Reformation. The first thesis put forth for disputation reads: "When our Lord and Master Jesus Christ said *Poenitentiam agite* [Repent], He willed the whole life of the faithful to be one of repentance."[5]

2. Translation mine. The Spanish original reads: "Eres tú José? ¿Tu esposa es María? Entren, peregrinos, no los conocía." See "En el nombre del cielo," #284 in *Libro de Liturgia y Cántico*.

3. Translation mine. The Spanish original reads: "Entren, santos peregrinos, peregrinos, reciban este rincón, no de esta pobre morada, sino de mi corazón." See "Entren, santos peregrinos," #286 in *Libro de Liturgia y Cántico*.

4. For an account of the toleration, demise, and popular reception of the fifteenth-century Spanish *villancico* still in use in Latin America today, see Laird, *Towards a History*; and Knighton and Torrente, eds., *Devotional Music*.

5. Translation mine. The original Latin reads: "Dominus et Magister noster Iesus Christus, dicendo poenitentiam agite etc. omnem vitam fidelium poenitentiam esse voluit."

In a Christmas Day sermon on Luke 2 from 1521, Luther brings hearers into the story of the Holy Family's struggle to find a welcoming reception for baby Jesus in Bethlehem. If we had been the innkeepers, would we have welcomed Mary and her baby into our hearts? The preacher uses the story as a mirror, so that people might see their own lack of hospitality towards pilgrims in their midst. Luther brings the text to life by calling hearers to repentance for failing to reach out to people like Mary and her baby, opening their eyes to see Christ in needy neighbors.

> There are many who are enkindled with dreamy devotion, when they hear of such poverty of Christ, are almost angry with the citizens of Bethlehem, denounce their blindness and ingratitude, and think, if they had been there, they would have shown the Lord and his mother a more becoming service, and would not have permitted them to be treated so miserably. But they do not look by their side to see how many of their fellow men need their help, and which they let go on in their misery unaided. Who is there upon earth that has no poor, miserable, sick erring ones, or sinful people around him? Why does he not exercise his love to those? Why does he not do to them as Christ has done to him? It is altogether false to think that you have done much for Christ, if you do nothing for those needy ones. Had you been at Bethlehem you would have paid as little attention to Christ as they did. . . . But now, you beat the air and do not recognize the Lord in your neighbor, you do not do to him as he has done to you.[6]

Parting from Christ's self-identification with the stranger and the apostolic teaching on hospitality, Lutherans have argued for the church's responsibility towards vulnerable neighbors, including the aliens in our midst. We see an example of such an approach to immigration law and reform in Stephen Bouman and Ralston Deffenbaugh's *They Are Us: Lutherans*

---

6. Martin Luther, "Christmas Day," 155. Similarly, Luther's explanation of the fifth commandment in his Large Catechism (1529) calls the faithful to see Christ in "those in need and peril of body and life." He writes: "Therefore God rightly calls all persons murderers who do not offer counsel or assistance to those in need and peril of body and life. He will pass a most terrible sentence upon them at the Last Day, as Christ himself says. He will say: 'I was hungry and you gave me food, I was thirsty and you gave me nothing to drink, I was a stranger and you did not welcome me, naked and you did not give me clothing, sick and in prison and you did not visit me.' That is to say, 'You would have permitted me and my family to die of hunger, thirst, and cold, to be torn to pieces by wild beasts, to rot in prison or perish from want.'" "Ten Commandments" in "The Large Catechism," para. 191, in Kolb and Wengert, eds., *Book of Concord*, 412.

and Immigration.[7] Using as their guiding principle the biblical teaching of evangelical hospitality, and reminding a historically immigrant Lutheran church in North America of its own immigrant roots, the authors argue for a preferential option of love for the strangers in our midst.

By focusing their attention on how immigrant neighbors are negatively affected by certain aspects of immigration law, Bouman and Deffenbaugh are able to identify ways in which the immigration system is at odds with values Christians hold in high esteem. They argue that the current immigration legal system is broken in such a way that families suffer extended separation from loved ones, unskilled workers who contribute to the economy receive inadequate compensation and unjust treatment, and people fleeing persecution or seeking a more dignified life are not always dealt with adequately.[8]

First, the backlog in processing visa applications (especially for people from Mexico) can often lead to years of separation from spouse and children.[9] Family unity suffers. Second, the annual number of immigrant visas for unskilled jobs not filled by the native-born is arguably too low to meet the actual demand for jobs in U.S. agricultural, service, and construction industries.[10] Failure to deal with the economic laws of supply and demand entice the poor to migrate for available economic opportunity, but also leads to unfair labor practices. Third, the authors consider the increased use of detention centers for vulnerable immigrants, including children, who pose no threat or danger to society, as an unnecessary and harsh form of treatment.[11] Apart from the merits of each of these examples of the brokenness of the system, it is clear that a commitment to the immigrant neighbor serves as the primary thematic lens for entering the immigration debate, providing a way to assess law and imagine workable solutions towards reform.

7. Bouman and Deffenbaugh, *They Are Us.*

8. Ibid., 59–69.

9. For instance, a lawful permanent resident (LPR) of the U.S. who did not enter the country with his or her spouse and minor children "must wait at least three years and nine months to be reunited with his or her spouse. . . . If the LPR is from Mexico, he or she must wait seven years and five months." Ibid., 60.

10. The authors note that "the demand for unskilled jobs that is not being filled by native-born workers is between 400,000 to 500,000 per year. Yet under current law, the annual number of immigrant visas for unskilled workers is only five-thousand." Ibid., 63.

11. The authors see the increasing use of detention centers for the great majority of low-risk asylum seekers as too drastic a form of enforcement. Ibid., 65.

What are the advantages of taking immigrant neighbors as a point of departure in immigration discussions? This approach certainly draws attention to their dignity as God's creatures, but also to their vulnerability, making them special objects of mercy and care. One is reminded of God's command to Israel: "You shall treat the stranger who sojourns with you as the native among you, and you shall love him as yourself, for you were strangers in the land of Egypt" (Lev 19:33–34). Echoing God's command, appeals to recall our country's or church's spiritual ancestors' immigrant past are made to prevent a certain historical amnesia about our forefathers' and foremothers' struggles, and are often used in calls for solidarity with modern-day aliens.[12] The focus on the church's hospitality towards the strangers in her midst functions to warn Christians against the casual or frequent use of uncharitable or harsh language against immigrants fueled by sensationalist media or discriminatory rhetoric.[13] Moreover, the concern for immigrant neighbors extends to the Christian's genuine interest in their spiritual wellbeing, their need for pastoral care, and welcoming reception in the church.

A commitment towards immigrant neighbors can be argued rhetorically through a creedal or Trinitarian hermeneutic (see figure 1 below).[14] Accordingly, Lutherans often start discussions on immigration with God's command for us to love the aliens in our midst as ourselves (1st article), Christ's example of self-identification with strangers in his ministry (2nd article), or the apostolic teaching on hospitality as an expression of the church's life in the Spirit (3rd article). While not exclusively Lutheran, the biblical basis for this creedal framework does reflect and is inspired by a basic commitment to the Reformation's principle of *sola scriptura*, namely, that Scripture alone stands as "the only rule and guiding principle according to which all teachings and teachers are to be evaluated and judged."[15]

12. Ibid., 25–53.

13. A report of the Commission on Theology and Church Relations of The Lutheran Church—Missouri Synod (LCMS), for which I served as the main drafter, makes this point. See *Immigrants Among Us*, 19.

14. Seeing themselves in continuity with the early church, Lutherans assume a creedal (and thus Trinitarian) hermeneutic for reading Scripture's witness to God's story of salvation in Christ. The Book of Concord of 1580, which comprises the confessional writings of the sixteenth-century Lutheran Reformers, begins with the Three Ecumenical Creeds. See Kolb and Wengert, eds., *Book of Concord*, 19–25.

15. "Epitome" of "Formula of Concord," para. 1, in Kolb and Wengert, eds., *Book of Concord*, 486; cf. ibid., para. 7, 487.

Indeed, no genuine Lutheran approach to ethical issues can do without a solid scriptural and creedal basis.

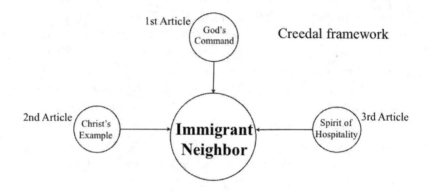

Love Thy Neighbor...

Legality-illegality, not a major issue

Figure 1

When seeing Christ in the vulnerable neighbor, the main concern is not the polarity of legality or illegality so prevalent in contemporary immigration talk. Not because discussions on the law are trivial, but because God's command to love alien neighbors is unconditional and thus not tied to the fulfillment of legal requirements. Adopting this foundational biblical commitment "suggests that legal or illegal status cannot be a prerequisite for the church's concern about the basic dignity of aliens and their families, their fair and just treatment in society, and their need to hear the Gospel and receive the sacraments."[16]

While genuine concern for immigrants can lead to reflections about the law's adequacy or lack thereof in dealing with them, Lutheran sources that promote the Christian's self-identification with needy neighbors do not automatically lead to such questions in the context of modern political realities such as the existence of nation-states and their commitment to their own citizens and residents. Be that as it may, the focus on God's command

---

16. Commission on Theology and Church Relations, *Immigrants Among Us*, 18.

to love the immigrant even apart from such important questions does offer Christians a moral compass for engaging the immigration debate today.

Living under God's Two Kingdoms: Luther's Pacifism and Ethics of Advocacy

As people of faith in God's promises, Christians are like father Abraham, who "not knowing where he was going," was called by God to migrate from his land to a foreign "land of promise . . . looking forward to the city . . . whose designer and builder is God" (Heb 11:8–10). Through faith in Christ, "our citizenship is in heaven" (Phil 3:20), so that before God and one another we "are no longer strangers and aliens," but "fellow citizens with the saints and members of the household of God" (Eph 2:19). Being citizens and residents of the city of God, Christians are called to "abstain from the passions of the flesh," acknowledging their identity in this world "as sojourners and exiles," as a "holy nation" called to live in accordance with God's "mercy" extended to them in Christ (1 Pet 2:9–11).

And yet Christians are also called by God to submit to temporal authorities "sent by him to punish those who do evil and to praise those who do good" (1 Pet 2:14). As residents of an earthly city, they are subject to "governing authorities" who have been "instituted" or "appointed" by God to "bear the sword" in accordance with God's "wrath" against injustice (Rom 13:1–7). Summing up these biblical teachings, the *Augsburg Confession* of 1530, one of the key confessional texts of the Lutheran Reformation, calls Christians "to be subject to political authority and to obey its commands and laws," even as it calls them to "obey God rather than human beings" (Acts 5:29) when "a command of the political authority cannot be followed without sin."[17]

In his treatise on *Temporal Authority* from 1523, Luther acknowledges this dual character and responsibility of the Christian as a member of both God's kingdom and the earthly kingdom. In the kingdom of Christ, the Gospel of the forgiveness of sins rules our human relationships and we need no law or government, "since Christians have in their heart the Holy Spirit, who both teaches and makes them to do injustice to no one, to love everyone, and to suffer injustice and even death willingly and cheerfully

17. *Confessio Augustana*, sec. XVI, para. 6–7, in Kolb and Wengert, eds., *Book of Concord*, 50.

at the hands of anyone."[18] Luther offers a pacifist ethics through which Christians deal with one another and their enemies with mercy and love, and thus without seeking justice or vengeance from the government for wrongdoings.

At the same time, Luther also acknowledges that earth is no paradise. Since people will use the freedom of the Gospel to justify sin whenever possible, the temporal sword has a place in this age to curb sin and punish evil. Wherever anyone attempts to rule the world by the Gospel in this present age, "there wickedness is given a free rein and the door is open for all manner of rascality."[19] Luther thus distinguishes between "two governments" or realms of God's activity in the world, which fulfill two distinct functions in our lives. The "spiritual" government is God's rule in the heart through the Holy Spirit and its purpose is "to produce righteousness," or to make one "righteous in the sight of God" through faith in Christ.[20] Its goal is the sinner's justification before God. The purpose of the "temporal government" is "to bring about external peace and prevent evil deeds."[21] God has established both governments for our good.

Reflecting on the Sermon on the Mount's words "Do not resist evil; but if anyone strikes you on the right cheek, turn to him the other also" (Matt 5:39), Luther makes a distinction between God's inward kingdom and the outward kingdom of the world. As individuals, Christians may indeed turn the other cheek when they are dealt with unfairly. Yet as collective members of society with responsibilities towards people other than themselves, Christians must make room for the law in the earthly kingdom, advocating for justice by restraining those who have wronged neighbors in the community.

> In the one case, you consider yourself and what is yours; in the other, you consider your neighbor and what is his. In what concerns you and yours, you govern yourself by the gospel and suffer injustice toward yourself as a true Christian; in what concerns the person or property of others, you govern yourself according to love and tolerate no injustice toward your neighbor.[22]

18. Martin Luther, "Temporal Authority," in *LW* 45:89.

19. Ibid., 92.

20. Ibid.

21. Ibid.

22. Ibid., 96.

Paradoxically, Luther asks us to hold two teachings in tension, asking us to live wisely under God's two kingdoms, or to "satisfy God's kingdom inwardly and the kingdom of the world outwardly."[23] In what concerns the inward kingdom, we may say that Luther espouses a form of "pacifist" ethics.[24] In what concerns the outward kingdom, however, he espouses an ethics of advocacy for those neighbors who have been wronged. As Luther puts it: "You suffer evil and injustice, and yet at the same time, you punish evil and injustice; you do not resist evil, and yet at the same time, you do resist it."[25]

In immigration debates, Lutherans have framed their thoughts in the context of the need for meeting responsibilities in the temporal kingdom. Some defend the duty of upholding the rule of law, including arguments for the rights of modern nation-states to regulate their borders. We see an example of this approach in political theorist Peter Meilaender's *Toward a Theory of Immigration*, where he proposes that the citizens of a nation have a right to define their own views of political community and national identity in the construction of immigration law.[26] Meilaender asks: "May (or perhaps must) we prefer 'our own'—our families, friends, neighbors, and compatriots, the shared way of life we develop together, even the familiar vistas of our native land—to other people, in different places, with different ways of life?"[27] While Bouman and Deffenbaugh invite Lutherans to see immigrant neighbors as one of us (thus their book title, "They Are Us") in light of our common dignity as God's creatures and immigrant past, Meilaender argues instead for a preferential option for one's fellow countrymen and women.

Meilaender is critical of public church statements that only speak about caring for the aliens in our midst without attending to policy considerations such as "the purposes of politics, relationships between insiders and outsiders, and the foundations of international order."[28] He agrees "that we owe something to each person simply by virtue of his or her humanity,"

---

23. Ibid.

24. "The Christian is also obliged to regard the Sermon on the Mount as the fundamental law, so to speak, of the new aeon with its radical, 'pacifist' ethics." Lohse, *Luther's Theology*, 321.

25. Martin Luther, "Temporal Authority," in *LW* 45:96.

26. Meilaender, *Theory of Immigration*.

27. Ibid., 3.

28. Amstutz and Meilaender, "Public Policy," 13.

but adds that "we also stand in particular relationships to certain persons for whom we bear special responsibilities," including "fellow citizens."[29] While giving priority to a nation's right to enforce its immigration laws, Meilaender cites two instances or non-absolute "exceptions" in which a government's right to define its policies "may nevertheless not simply be a matter that each nation is entirely free to determine for itself."[30] He lists assistance to refugees ("the truly desperate") and unification of close family members ("family unity") as morally compelling transnational duties or "values that circumscribe states' freedom of action."[31]

One of the advantages of Luther's teaching on the two kingdoms is its demand for engaging temporal law on its own terms without using the Gospel as a trump card to evade or preempt such discussion. While Bouman/Deffenbaugh and Meilaender approach immigration issues from different places, they both deal directly at some point with the state of the law. Bouman and Deffenbaugh engage law as a way to reveal the immigration system's brokenness and the need to fix it in order to deal fairly with alien neighbors. Meilaender argues for immigration law to justify the need for a system that gives priority to its own citizens while being open to sensible policies dealing with foreign nationals.[32] While the potential danger for using Luther's distinction between the two kingdoms to justify a temporal government's unjust *status quo* exists, the distinction calls Christians to actually care about the state of the law, debate and even disagree on various aspects of it, and work to make laws better as much as they are able. Far from being an affront to the rule of law, such critical and non-violent Christian political engagement can indeed reflect a true respect for the rule of law and God's gift of temporal government.[33]

29. Meilaender, "Immigration," 11.

30. Meilaender, *Theory of Immigration*, 173.

31. Ibid., 174, 180.

32. In political ethical discourse, Meilaender gives priority to "the moral legitimacy of regimes" (e.g., the U.S. system of government) that citizens pledge allegiance to in general, over "specific policy issues" (e.g., U.S. immigration law) that citizens may or may not agree with in every respect. See Amstutz and Meilaender, "Public Policy," 14.

33. Commission on Theology and Church Relations, *Immigrants Among Us*, 25–26. It follows that Christians will react differently to the state of the law. Some may determine that, while not perfect, the law is fine as it stands. Others will dramatize injustice through public protests. Others will allow peaceful coexistence with non-threatening undocumented neighbors, while waiting for legal remedies or comprehensive immigration reform. See ibid., 22, 32–33.

Luther's distinction has also been used in appeals for maintaining the church's role in the spiritual kingdom undisturbed from political considerations. While at first this move towards distinction seems to encourage separation from political engagement, this need not be the case. Each Christian can work to make laws better and collaborate with other like-minded individuals to do so. Still we are faced with the reality that not all Christians will agree on the moral failure of immigration laws. Christians are called to obey the authorities, and the laws they enact, unless such laws are against God's law. But *when* exactly is this or that immigration law or policy explicitly against God's command? In dealing with such questions, genuine diversity of opinion is inevitable even among Christians who share a common confession. We are thus reminded that politics cannot dictate the church's evangelical identity and mission in the world.

Therefore, I have argued that the Lutheran distinction between the two kingdoms encourages the church to ground her unity in the Gospel alone and carry out her God-ordained evangelical mission to give spiritual care and extend the hand of mercy to undocumented immigrants in spite of her members' individual positions on immigration law or policy.[34] A salutary contribution of the Lutheran distinction between temporal and spiritual governments is that it allows for disagreement on political issues without letting such disagreements get in the way of the church's unity and mission in the world.

Just as Luther's distinction can lead Christians to take seriously their identity as citizens of the state who care about the law, it can also lead them to take to heart their Gospel-rooted identity as citizens of heaven who are one in Christ and are called by God to invite all people regardless of legal status into the church.

> Affirming God's action in both realms allows us to disagree with other Christians on immigration law without destroying our unity in Christ. The unity of the church is anchored in the Gospel and not in this or that law. . . . [A]ffirming God's governing in both realms helps us to acknowledge the duty of every citizen (or resident) to obey the law without letting such duty affect negatively his commitment to promote the proclamation of the Gospel and the works of mercy that ultimately define the church's mission to all without distinction.[35]

34. Sánchez M., "Misión e inmigración," 74.
35. Ibid.

By making a distinction between temporal and spiritual matters, Lutheran theology allows us to live as citizens of the state under God's command to obey the authorities, and as citizens of heaven under Christ's command to make disciples of all nations. Living in God's world entails serving neighbors in both areas of activity, each with its own goal. The temporal kingdom seeks to promote *justice* between various sets of neighbors through the law as a means of establishing a certain measure—though by no means a perfect one—of civil peace, order, and righteousness in society. It encourages Christian concern for working towards adequate laws without resorting to violence. The spiritual realm promotes *justification* before God through faith in Christ, and thus Christian concern for the preaching of the Gospel to all without distinction (see figure 2 below). God rules and preserves the world through His work in both kingdoms.

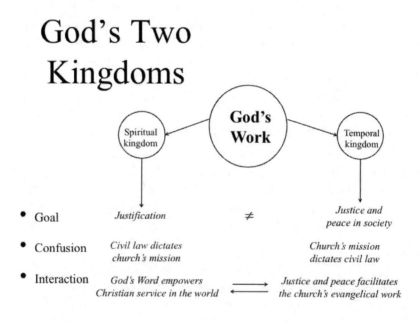

Figure 2

As our illustration shows, confusion between the aims of both kingdoms arises, for instance, when Christians argue that God's universal commands to love the neighbor or preach the Gospel to all nations stand as higher laws that trump in an absolute way a temporal state's responsibility to create, enact, and enforce immigration laws. Indeed, Christians can rightly use these commands as moral principles to guide their assessment and critique of laws they deem inadequate or unjust for various sets of neighbors. This form of interaction between the two kingdoms is possible, since God's Word empowers Christians to work with neighbors for justice in society. However, interaction is different than making the church act as (or supplant) a secular government with its own immigration laws. The church's evangelical mission is neither to enact civil law nor to replace the temporal government.

Confusion between the two kingdoms also happens when Christians act or talk as if undocumented immigrants cannot be true Christians because of their legal status. The same attitude may lead to timid or non-existent efforts on the part of the church to reach out to immigrant neighbors with humanitarian aid, evangelistic initiatives, pastoral care, and theological formation. While the church as a legal temporal entity must take care to abide by government regulations (e.g., in labor practices), the government must not interfere with the church's spiritual duty to love alien neighbors regardless of their legal status. Justice and peace in the land can indeed facilitate the church's mission, giving free course to the preaching and teaching of the Gospel, but civil law does not dictate the church's mission. Again, the two kingdoms interact, but each has its own legitimate aims.

In the temporal government, the Christian acts as a "world-person" and applies an ethics of advocacy for various sets of neighbors who seek justice.[36] As a "world-person," the Christian does not turn the other cheek and suffers injustice, but actively advocates for justice on behalf of others. A certain complexity ensues because such neighbors may include immigrants, but also citizens and residents of a nation. Matters such as human rights, labor practices, supply and demand economics, and border security become important considerations. When it comes to the spiritual kingdom, however, the Christian acts as a "Christ-person" and sees all neighbors without distinction as people for whom Christ died.[37] Here there are no borders. The Christian shares the Gospel, offers relief, and shows hospitality to undocumented immigrants without placing legal requirements or conditions upon them.

36. Lohse, *Luther's Theology*, 321.
37. Ibid.

Attending to God's Calling(s): Towards an Ethics of Vocation

In his *Treatise on Good Works* from 1520, Luther attacks the popular medieval distinction between spiritual and earthly works. Some think that good works "consist only of praying in church, fasting, and almsgiving," but in reality "God is served by all things that may be done, spoken, or thought in faith."[38] God's commandments establish what good works are.[39] Because Christians are bound to God's commands by faith, there are no special distinctions among believers or their works. Luther states: "In this faith all works become equal, and one work is like the other; all distinctions between works fall away, whether they be great, small, short, long, many, or few."[40] How does one become rich in good works? Luther notes that if each Christian were to fulfill his or her calling, "office, and attend to its duties alone," good works would abound.[41] Christians exercise such offices and duties in the estates or orders of marriage, church, and government.

In his *Small Catechism* of 1529, Luther included a Table of Duties, where he lists "all kinds of holy orders and walks of like" through which Christians serve neighbors.[42] Luther uses the term "holy orders" consciously as an implicit critique of the prevalent medieval idea that the monastic orders alone were to be seen as "holy" and therefore as superior to other Christians' more lowly works. The Table includes the duties of bishops, pastors, and preachers (ecclesial order); governing authorities (political order); as well as husbands, wives, parents, children, male and female servants, day laborers, workers, etc. (economic order, which includes the household). A mother's work to nurse a child is no less "holy" than a bishop's work of teaching the faith.

Similarly, in the conclusion of the Ten Commandments in his *Large Catechism* of 1529, Luther speaks against any notion of holiness that is tied to self-designed works instead of the quotidian works that flow naturally from God's commands. If Christians were to concentrate on their "everyday domestic duties of one neighbor to another," which have the command

---

38. Martin Luther, "Treatise on Good Works," in *LW* 44:24.

39. Ibid., 23.

40. Ibid., 26.

41. Ibid., 99.

42. "The Household Chart of Some Bible Passages" in "The Small Catechism," para. 2, in Kolb and Wengert, eds., *Book of Concord*, 365.

of God, rather than in inventing their own "showy" works, "you will surely find so much to do that you will neither seek nor pay attention to any other works or other kind of holiness."[43] Christians are encouraged to fulfill joyfully their God-given callings or vocations in the estates or orders God has already placed them in.

The Lutheran teaching on vocation provides yet another thematic lens to approach the immigration debate. Its point of departure is God's calling to each Christian, his or her vocation in the world, which defines the particular neighbors they have been called to serve and defend. By exercising their vocations, all Christians serve as "masks of God" in the world, as the means through which God blesses many neighbors.[44] Indeed, the law of God calls us to love our neighbor as ourselves. But what does that concretely look like? If everybody is my neighbor, then, nobody is my neighbor. There are too many neighbors around the world. As God's creatures, we have neither the time nor the energy to get to all of them. It would be impossible. By narrowing the scope of neighbors, vocation is liberating and makes the fulfillment of the law of love realistic.[45]

Vocation makes God's command to love a concrete reality in the face of each neighbor we have been called to serve in different spheres of influence. We begin with our closest neighbors at home, moving towards neighbors at church, work, and school, and then considering also other neighbors such as fellow citizens and the strangers with needs outside of our immediate circles (see figure 3 below). Vocation places us in a web

---

43. "Ten Commandments" in "The Large Catechism," para. 313, 318, in Kolb and Wengert, eds., *Book of Concord*, 428–29; "Many examples are recorded of people leaving wife and child—even their civil office—and putting themselves in a monastery. This, they said, is fleeing from the world and seeking a life that is more pleasing to God than the other life. They were unable to realize that one should serve God by observing the commandments he has given and not through the commandments contrived by human beings." *Confessio Augustana*, sec. XXVII, para. 56–58, in Kolb and Wengert, eds., *Book of Concord*, 90.

44. "Instead of coming in uncovered majesty when he gives a gift to man, God places a mask before his face. He clothes himself in the form of an ordinary man who performs his work on earth. Human beings are to work, 'everyone according to his vocation and office,' through this they serve as masks of God, behind which he can conceal himself when he would scatter his gifts." Wingren, *Luther on Vocation*, 138.

45. "The Decalogue and the commandment of love do not give very definite or detailed instructions about what we as individuals ought to do here and now in living together with one another. This commandment of love, valid everywhere and for all people, becomes specific for us as individuals in the context of the station in life in which God has placed us." Althaus, *Ethics of Martin Luther*, 36.

of human relationships with various degrees of responsibilities towards neighbors. Indeed, the law of God is changeless in and of itself, and therefore "represents unchanging imitation," but the command of love has to be contextualized in the present tense and thus "calls man to his vocation, which is guided by the need of 'the time.'"[46] By focusing on neighbors from our particular vocational locations, the weight of the whole world is no longer on our shoulders. Vocation is thus experienced as a divine blessing and joyful task.

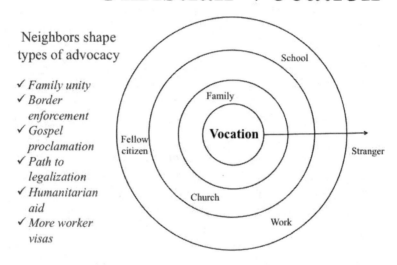

Christian Vocation

Neighbors shape
types of advocacy

✓ *Family unity*
✓ *Border enforcement*
✓ *Gospel proclamation*
✓ *Path to legalization*
✓ *Humanitarian aid*
✓ *More worker visas*

Family

Vocation

Fellow citizen

Stranger

School

Church

Work

Figure 3

Vocation allows us to argue boldly on behalf of some neighbor, coming to his or her defense. Bouman and Deffenbaugh's advocacy for comprehensive immigration reform (meaning an approach that is not only enforcement-based) flows from their vocational location, including a lifetime of work among immigrants and refugees. Bouman served as director of Evangelical Outreach and Congregational Mission for the

---

46. "The law does not consider changing situations, but the command is addressed to the present need. In a way, the law represents unchanging imitation, without regard for 'the time,' but the command calls man to his vocation, which is guided by the need of 'the time.'" Wingren, *Luther on Vocation*, 233.

Evangelical Lutheran Church in America (ELCA), and Deffenbaugh served as president of Lutheran Immigration and Refugee Service (LIRS). Their God-given callings to work among these neighbors over many years rightly compel them to speak on their behalf. Meilaender implies the idea of vocation by appealing to "special relationships" in his argument for the priority of fellow citizens over foreign nationals in the enactment of immigration laws.[47] He argues that a special proximity to neighbors with whom we share the common bond of nationhood establishes a certain priority to take care of their needs first, before addressing those of other neighbors.

Because we are faced with so many neighbors asking for our attention, vocation helps us to define *who* are our closest neighbors, but also what neighbors' needs we should deal with *first*, and *how* to do so. Neighbors shape types of advocacy. Vocational location explains to some extent why Christians with an equal commitment to the command to love the neighbor give different weight to various factors in immigration reform. These factors include Gospel proclamation, labor demand and worker visas, national security and border enforcement, family unity and unification, and earned path to legalization. Vocational priorities guide various forms of advocacy on behalf of different neighbors.

Interestingly, Meilaender makes room in his approach for attending to other neighbors who are not fellow citizens, but whose plight deserves serious consideration. Beyond refugees and separated families, Meilaender has advocated for those immigrants who have become *de facto* our neighbors and part of our communities, and argues for possibly providing amnesty to them as long as certain legal conditions are fulfilled such as "the payment of back taxes or proficiency in English."[48] The implication is that there are neighbors who, though originally seen as strangers living farther away from our circles, have actually become over time members of our community and therefore one of us.

Luther does not understand vocation in an exclusivist sense, since the law of God also commands us to love neighbors outside of our particular vocations as opportunities arise.[49] We serve those who are closest to us first, but then also make room for others. Yet those "other" neighbors eventually

47. Meilaender, "Immigration," 11.

48. Ibid., 12. Nevertheless, Meilaender does not appear to acknowledge data showing that undocumented workers actually pay taxes, contributing to Medicare and the Social Security Administration's "earning suspense file," from which they will get no benefit. See Solana, "Illegal Immigrants."

49. See Althaus, *Ethics of Martin Luther*, 41.

also become closer to us, becoming members of our own families, churches, and labor networks. At that point, there is an unavoidable proximity that raises the question of our responsibilities towards these neighbors too. When immigrant neighbors "out there" are seen and live as immigrant neighbors "among us," we expand our circle of neighbors and reshape our vocational focus.

Conclusion: Rhetorical Strategies in the Immigration Debate

Our Lutheran frameworks for thinking through immigration issues can serve as rhetorical devices for engaging in conversation with others. Some Christians argue almost solely from the perspective of Christ's self-identification with strangers. *What part of "love your neighbor as yourself" do you not understand?* Others tend to focus only on obedience to authorities and the laws they enact. *What part of "obey the authorities" do you not understand?* Still others argue from the perspective of the church's call to share the Gospel with neighbors from all nations? *What part of "go and make disciples" do you not understand?* Without recognizing the diversity of vantage points Christians adopt to discuss what is often a highly debated topic, we are likely to talk past each other. No one theme sufficiently captures every aspect of the debate. Yet it is quite helpful to know where people are coming from, before getting them to see that there is more to consider. Learning to see the same issue from different angles should enrich our conversations.

Each framework offers its own contribution to the debate. As an example, each framework deals with the problem of the law from different angles. God's command to love the neighbor, including the immigrant, raises questions about the use of biblical texts that call Christians to obey the civil authorities and the laws they enact. How does one reconcile these demands to obey the authorities with God's command to love the strangers? Moreover, the distinction between God's work in the world through the law in the temporal realm leads us to ask how Christians should respond to civil laws that are not adequate, how the temporal and spiritual kingdoms should interact with one another, and what might be the consequences of confusing the two kingdoms or governments when approaching immigration issues.

The affirmation of a Christian's particular vocation(s) to serve specific neighbors in society offers a concrete context for fulfilling God's law, but also raises questions about the nature and scope of our responsibilities towards other neighbors who might not fall neatly within our vocations. How does one deal with "other" neighbors that at first seem to be far from us, and yet are all around us? Are they taking care of our children, making our meals, cutting our lawns, building our businesses, or picking up our fruits and vegetables? If so, when do those strangers and their children become *de facto* one of us, members of our families, schools, churches, and work networks? What then are our responsibilities towards those neighbors? What laws would best acknowledge their contributions to our common way of life? What forms of advocacy follow from such acknowledgment?

Each framework may work better than another given the audience and types of questions one is trying to answer. When encountering a Christian who asks, "what part of 'obey the authorities' do you not understand?" we have an opportunity to talk seriously about law, including those aspects of immigration law that may reveal a broken system. Respect for government and the rule of law does not mean blind trust in government, but an honest and critical approach to those laws that may not be working. This is especially the case in a representative democracy, where citizens have a right to debate these issues and use the power of the vote and other advocacy means to change laws that might not be adequate, fair, or comprehensive enough to deal with complex issues. A respectful yet critical attitude in the temporal kingdom can strengthen the rule of law over time, so that it can provide a greater measure of peace and justice in society in the long run. Moreover, Christians who are too focused on temporal kingdom matters can be encouraged to think more seriously about their responsibilities to others as members of the spiritual kingdom.

When dealing with someone who asks, "what part of 'go and make disciples' do you not understand?" we have an opportunity to engage questions about our duties towards strangers in our communities who have not heard the Gospel, seek spiritual guidance, or can benefit from our humanitarian assistance. Similarly, Christians who ask, "what part of 'love the neighbor as yourself' do you not understand?" show they are especially concerned about the wellbeing of vulnerable neighbors. In these cases, starting with God's work in the spiritual kingdom or the immigrant neighbor becomes profitable for affirming the church's evangelical mission in the world and the Christian's call to be charitable to all people without distinction. At the same time, Christians who are too focused on these matters can be further encouraged to consider how their concerns for neighbors in need of daily bread as well as bread from heaven translate into forms of advocacy in God's temporal kingdom. If members of my congregation are undocumented immigrants, does not my unconditional love for them in Christ lead me to ask how I can advocate for them so that their legal status might be changed? Will I be willing to sacrifice time and resources to help my neighbor, whenever possible, with the necessary paperwork, translation, and legal advice to bring him or her out of the shadows?

Our diversity of Lutheran themes or narrative frameworks highlights not only that immigration is a complex reality that can be approached from several angles, but that Lutheran theology itself—due in part to its rich paradoxical character—can deal with such complexity theologically in a way that does not seek to resolve all tensions. Lutheran theology is willing to live with a certain measure of freedom and ambiguity in the realm of ethics, while also attempting to address issues practically for the sake of some neighbor in God's world as seen from the calling or vocation God has given each one to work with in this life. Without some neighbor in mind, calls to see Christ in the vulnerable stranger, debates about just law in God's temporal kingdom, missiological agendas about bringing Christ to the nations, and appeals to live out one's vocations in the world, mean little to nothing.[50] Whatever starting point one uses in approaching immigration issues today, a Lutheran ethic will ultimately force us to put a human face on the debate and lead us to ask, "Who is my neighbor?"

Discussion Questions

1. Can you summarize briefly the three Lutheran themes or frameworks for approaching immigration issues? See figures 1, 2, and 3 above for a quick review. Which one of the three starting points do you find most useful? In what way(s)?

2. Can you mention some ways in which undocumented immigrants are or can become vulnerable neighbors? How does Luther's sermon about the story of pregnant Mary's search for an inn for baby Jesus, or the Hispanic celebration of *Las Posadas*, help you to remember the vulnerable strangers in your community? How does this story affect you?

50. Sánchez M., "Human Face of Justice," 117–32.

3. Luther's teaching on the two kingdoms reminds us that we are citizens of an earthly government (temporal kingdom) and citizens of the heavenly city (spiritual kingdom). What are some Christian values you hold as a citizen of heaven? How do these values or principles inform your judgments about ethical issues (including immigration laws) in the temporal kingdom?

4. Which issues do you tend to advocate for the most in immigration debates (see figure 3 above for a list of issues)? In advocating for these issues, which neighbors are you looking out for or trying to defend? Is there something you can learn from people who advocate for different issues and neighbors in their approaches to immigration?

5. Which one of the three Lutheran frameworks for approaching immigration issues do you use more often in your own thinking or speaking about immigration? Mention one way in which a different starting point can complement or enrich your typical way of understanding or talking about immigration law and reform.

——— 3 ———

Calvin's Legacy of Compassion

A Reformed Theological Perspective on Immigration

Rubén Rosario Rodríguez

Introduction

AN ENDURING CHARACTERISTIC OF the Christian religion is its sense of
social responsibility in caring for the poor. The New Testament describes
Jesus' ministry as one of compassion and inclusivity, portraying Jesus as
a public figure unafraid to transcend cultural and religious norms for the
sake of a single individual's material and spiritual well-being. The religion
he inspired and founded consequently distinguished itself through communal practices of hospitality targeting the neighbor in need. Reformed
theology in the twenty-first century, inheritors of John Calvin's reformation
efforts in sixteenth-century Geneva, also recognizes this civic dimension of
the Christian faith. By focusing on Calvin's ministry in Geneva—a French
exile ministering to refugees from France, Poland, Spain, England, and
Italy—the Reformed theological tradition can identify valuable resources
for engaging the contemporary public debate over questions of immigration and social welfare.

Douglas Ottati describes Reformed theology in a "Calvinist key" as "a
theology that backs robust participation in the public realm" over against
the theology of sixteenth-century Anabaptist writers who considered civil
government "outside Christ."[1] In his *Institutes of the Christian Religion*, John
Calvin argues that God has established civil government so "that humanity

1. Ottati, "Reformed Theology," 449.

may be maintained among men,"[2] and views magistrates as the divinely appointed protectors and guardians of public well-being, "a calling, not only lawful before God, but also the most sacred and by far the most honorable of all callings, in the whole life of mortal men" (4.20.6). Accordingly, Calvin's discussion of civil government falls under the broader rubric of the Christian life, in which temporal governments exist "to cherish and protect the outward worship of God, to defend sound doctrine of piety, and the position of the church, to adjust our life to the society of men, to form our social behavior to civil righteousness, to reconcile us with one another, and to promote general peace and tranquility" (4.20.2). It follows that there are preferable forms of government—Calvin spoke out against unchecked, unilateral governance (4.20.8)—and that, despite a clear division of labor between *spiritual* (church) and *temporal* (state) governments, the temporal "establishment of civil justice and outward morality" (4.20.1) is grounded in and springs from "that spiritual and inward Kingdom of Christ, so we must know that they are not at variance. For spiritual government, indeed, is already initiating in us upon earth certain beginnings of the Heavenly Kingdom, and in this mortal and fleeting life affords a certain forecast of an immortal and incorruptible blessedness" (4.20.2). By this understanding, neither the church nor the state represent perfect and holy communities, but both are mixed societies of saints and sinners, elect and reprobate, making it necessary to acknowledge certain ambiguities and tensions within both spiritual and temporal governance.

This distinctly Calvinist view of human societies "recognizes that, even as they pursue their legitimate callings, politicians, lawyers, professors, business persons, and the rest will be implicated in the injustices and corruptions that mar all human societies."[3] While all human institutions, the church included, are continually in need of repentance and reform, Reformed theologies descended from Calvin also believe "in confidence in the divine provision for justice and for good."[4] Accordingly, theological voices belong in the public discourse—even when advocating separation of church and state as Calvin did—in order to ensure that the fundamental Christian obligation of compassion toward those in need is properly car-

2. Calvin, *Institutes*, 4.20.3. Subsequent references to *Institutes* will be made in parenthesis in the text. While committed to using gender-inclusive language throughout this work, all quotations reflect the culturally and historically bound perspectives of the original author.

3. Ottati, "Reformed Theology," 451.

4. Ibid.

ried out. For Calvin, and those traditions influenced by Calvin, the establishment of a just social order is part and parcel of the Christian life. The call to minister to the poor, the sick, the widow, the orphan, the refugee, and the prisoner (Matt 25:34–40) is a matter of concern for both church and state because it is first and foremost a spiritual concern for all Christians: "take as strong a stand against evil as we can. This command is given to everyone not only to princes, magistrates, and officers of justice, but to all private persons as well."[5]

Focusing on issues of immigration, especially immigration reform in the U.S. context, the emphasis of a Calvinist, Reformed theological perspective is the preservation of basic human dignity through the church's various ministries while advocating for equally compassionate policies in the temporal realm. Three loci help center a discussion of John Calvin as a resource for contemporary Reformed theological reflection on immigration:

1. Calvin's experience as a refugee, exile, and resident alien in Geneva;

2. Genevan ministries of compassion, specifically diaconal ministries like the General Hospital, whose main purpose was to relieve poverty among native Genevans, and the *Bourse française* (or French Fund), established to address the severe problems caused by immigration; and

3. Calvin's discussion of the Christian life in book three of the *Institutes*, in which this life is a journey and the "earth is but our place of exile" (3.9.4).

Following this brief overview of Calvin's theological response to the problems of political and economic migration, the conclusion applies insights gained from this legacy of Christian compassion to the contemporary U.S. discussion on reforming immigration policies.

Calvin the Exile and Resident Alien

Recent works have examined the role of Calvin's personal experience as a political refugee and a Protestant pastor living in exile on Calvin's theological writing, in order to argue that this experience of displacement cannot be ignored when examining the full impact of his theology for contemporary

5. Calvin, *Sermons on 2 Samuel*, 419.

Reformed theology.[6] Historian Heiko Oberman makes this observation about Calvin's view of the reforming church as a transcultural, transnational entity in sixteenth-century Europe: "Calvin discovered the ecumenical church at his conversion . . . But in Strasbourg he discovered a new mark of the church (*nota ecclesiae*): the authentic church of Christ, like the people of the Jews, is persecuted and dispersed."[7] While methodologically, Calvin the theologian did not rank autobiography and personal experience high on his list of theological sources, the fact remains that his life was indelibly marked by the experience of political persecution and displacement. Nowhere is this more evident than in the proliferation of social welfare ministries in Calvin's Geneva, which became a haven for Protestant refugees fleeing persecution from throughout Roman Catholic Europe. Historian Carter Lindberg argues that Geneva was not merely a port in the storm for the victims of persecution, but that Geneva's highly successful example of a Christian society built upon Protestant principles instigated further migration: "Geneva not only welcomed refugees, it created them. At the center of all the praise and blame that swirled through and around Geneva stood John Calvin, himself a displaced person from France."[8]

While John Calvin did not formally acknowledge his own refugee experience in the work of biblical exegesis and doctrinal theology, throughout his exegetical work numerous references can be found expressing concern for the resident alien, intentionally focusing the Christian life toward creating "a just and well-regulated government [that] will be distinguished for maintaining the rights of the poor and afflicted."[9] So for Calvin, the chief task of doctrinal theology is biblical exegesis, but this process of exegesis uncovers certain inescapable demands on the Christian community regarding the poor and powerless, as demonstrated by these comments on Ps 82:3: "for those who are exposed an easy prey to the cruelty and wrongs of the rich have no less need of the assistance and protection of magistrates than the sick have of the aid of the physician. Were the truth deeply fixed

6. See the statement of consultation, World Alliance of Reformed Churches, "Economic and Social Witness," 3–7; Naphy, "Calvin's Geneva," 25–38; and Vosloo, "Displaced Calvin," 35–52. Vosloo draws extensively upon historian Heiko Oberman's controversial collection of essays, *Two Reformations*, in which Oberman examines the cultural, theological, and political legacy of Martin Luther and John Calvin, in order to establish Calvin's view of the church as a persecuted and dispersed community.

7. Oberman, *Two Reformations*, 148; cited by Vosloo in "Displaced Calvin," 41.

8. Lindberg, *European Reformations*, 249.

9. Calvin, *Calvin's Commentaries*, 5:332.

in the minds of kings and other judges, that they are appointed to be the guardians of the poor, and that a special part of this duty lies in resisting the wrongs which are done to them, and in repressing all unrighteous violence, perfect righteousness would become triumphant through the whole world."[10] It is under this biblical call to establish God's justice that Geneva, under John Calvin's pastoral care, became not only a refuge for persecuted Protestants, but also a beacon for reformers throughout Europe who came to Geneva to learn under Calvin in order to replicate his successes back home. The French formed the single largest ethnic enclave, though Italian, German, and even English refugees flooded into Geneva, not all desiring permanent residence, as evidenced by John Knox's brief stay from 1555 to 1558. However, this brief sojourn in Calvin's Geneva had such an effect on Knox that it contributed directly to the rapid spread of Calvinism throughout the English-speaking world. Of Calvin's reforms in Geneva, Knox writes: "I neither fear nor eschame to say, [it] is the most perfect school of Christ that ever was in the earth since the days of the apostles. In other places I confess Christ to be truly preached; but manners and religion so sincerely reformed, I have not yet seen in any other place."[11]

It is not surprising then, that upon John Calvin's return to Geneva after three years in Strasbourg (1538–1541) following his earlier expulsion, Calvin was invited to write not just the rules of church governance for the Genevan Church (what became the *Ecclesiastical Ordinances* of 1541), but also "was responsible for leading the committee to write what would become Geneva's first, postrevolutionary constitution."[12] Therefore, despite strong dislike for Calvin personally, as evidenced by repeated references to him as "that Frenchman" (*ille Gallus*) in the city council minutes, it says much about their estimation of Calvin's skills and abilities that in 1541, "this foreigner only recently returned from exile was given so great a role" in the reformation of both the Genevan church and its civil government.[13] One of the lessons Calvin learned during his three years in Strasbourg as the minister of a French refugee congregation was the importance of having a well-organized and unified church structure. While in Strasbourg, Calvin benefitted from contact with German reformer Martin Bucer, an advocate of Protestant unity, and many of the reforms Calvin later implemented

10. Ibid.
11. Knox, *Works of John Knox*, 4:240.
12. Naphy, "Calvin's Church in Geneva," 102.
13. Ibid.

in Geneva—especially those concerning ecclesiology and church governance—were originally developed in Strasbourg.[14] Ironically, while never
fully welcomed as one of their own, it was Calvin's experience as a refugee,
first in Geneva, briefly in Strasbourg, then again in Geneva until his death,
that most informed the church order Calvin implemented in Geneva. T. H.
L. Parker's biography of Calvin identifies this sojourn in Strasbourg as particularly positive and influential: "A happy situation for him; a Frenchman
among Frenchman, a refugee among refugees, a poor man among generally
poor men."[15]

The period of ecclesiastical reformation in sixteenth-century Geneva
was characterized by substantial dislocation and migration of various
populations as a result of religious persecution and warfare. While the Genevan authorities initially drove out many Catholics, many more Protestant
refugees were attracted to Geneva during Calvin's second stay, due to the
popularity of his preaching and the success of his church and civil reforms.
In other words, while many of the charitable institutions that cared for the
poor and provided relief to migrant populations predated Calvin's arrival
in Geneva, their long-term success benefitted from Calvin's reorganization
of church and civil governance. Historical demographers estimate that the
population of Geneva grew between 1550 and 1560—the most active decade of Calvin's ministry in Geneva—as high as 21,400 from 13,100, "an
increase of more than 60%."[16] Needless to say, this overwhelming influx
of refugees exacerbated the city's already strained social welfare infrastruc-
ture. An estimated 5 percent of Geneva's native population received regular
assistance from the General Hospital (about 500 people); add to that the
steady stream of displaced refugees (not all settled in Geneva but merely
passed through), and Geneva's social welfare agencies would likely serve an
additional 10,000 strangers during any one-year period.[17]

During these turbulent years, Calvin began to lecture on the Psalms
to an audience increasingly composed of refugees, and eventually com-
pleted his *Commentary on the Psalms* in 1557, at the height of Protestant
migration into Geneva. Therefore, it is not unrealistic to assume that the
plight of persecuted Protestants throughout Europe—but especially in his
native France—informed Calvin's exegesis of the Psalms. H. J. Selderhuis

14. van't Spijker, "Bucer's Influence on Calvin," 37–41.

15. Parker, *John Calvin*, 68.

16. Cited in Kingdon, "Calvinism and Social Welfare," 223.

17. Naphy, "Calvin's Church in Geneva," 114–15.

characterizes John Calvin as a refugee ministering to other refugees, and is not surprised to find within Calvin's *Commentary on the Psalms* repeated references to the themes of "exile" and "asylum."[18] Thus, Calvin's autobiographical sensitivity to the plight of persecuted and displaced Protestants resonates throughout his exegesis of the Psalms, yet is always placed within the explicit theological framework of the Christian life as a pilgrimage on this earth. In comparing the Protestant churches to Israel, Calvin reminds persecuted Protestants that the Children of God in David's Psalms are distinguished

> for the trial of their faith; for he speaks of them, not as *righteous* or *godly,* but as those that *wait upon the Lord.* What purpose would this waiting serve, unless they groaned under the burden of the cross? Moreover, the possession of the earth which he promises to the children of God is not always realized to them; because it is the will of the Lord that they should live as strangers and pilgrims in it; neither does he permit them to have any fixed abode in it, but rather tries them with frequent troubles, that they may desire with greater alacrity the everlasting dwelling-place of heaven.[19]

Social Welfare Ministries in Geneva

In the Middle Ages, Christian care of the poor centered around two social practices: (1) begging and almsgiving, and (2) public hospitals. Begging was the primary way in which the poor were assisted, and almsgiving was a significant component of personal piety within the sacramental system of salvation, since beggars were regarded as holy persons in the medieval theology of almsgiving, in which the almsgiver sees "the face of Christ in the beggar."[20] Despite theological support for begging, and the rise of the mendicant orders that incorporated begging into their ascetic rule, begging became a public nuisance and criminal enterprise in many cities. Most European cities of the late Middle Ages began to look for alternatives to begging and almsgiving as the primary means of caring for the poor, leading to the creation of public hospitals.

Unlike hospitals in the modern age, hospitals in the late medieval period did not just provide care for the sick, but were more like social welfare

18. See Selderhuis, *John Calvin,* 85–109.

19. Calvin, *Calvin's Commentaries,* 5:25–26: Ps 37:7–11.

20. Kingdon, "Calvinism and Social Welfare," 213.

institutions providing general care for the poor through various ministries of "hospitality." Some hospitals were large and cared for hundreds of guests, but most were small, private residences bequeathed by a wealthy patron at death for the purpose of caring for the poor: "In this house would live a priest, who would say masses for the souls of the dead donors and direct the activities of the hospital with the assistance of one or two servants."[21] A dozen or so people in need—elderly widows, orphans, men physically unable to work—would also live in the house. This practice eventually spread to all the major cities of Europe so that by the time of the Protestant Reformation, "most municipalities depended on a combination of regulated begging and hospitals to meet the needs of their poor."[22] Eventually, with the rapid growth of cities in the fifteenth century, these efforts proved insufficient to meet the needs of the poor, as evidenced by a 1531 imperial edict from the Holy Roman Emperor, Charles V, implementing reform of poor relief practices in the Low Countries, based on municipal reforms successfully implemented in Catholic cities like Mons and Ypres.[23] These reforms emphasized a move toward lay control of social welfare ministries and more prudent financial administration, often calling on prominent business leaders to administer hospitals, as opposed to the previous practice of having clergy, without business training or acumen, manage poor relief. Similar reforms in Geneva's social welfare ministries predated John Calvin's arrival, suggesting that while the "spread of this movement for laicized and rationalized welfare reform coincided almost precisely with the spread of the Protestant Reformation," Geneva's contributions to poor relief were part of a larger, humanist movement that encompassed Protestant and Catholic reformers.[24]

Nevertheless, it cannot be refuted that under John Calvin's leadership Geneva instituted such innovative reforms in church organization and civil governance that Geneva became a "model of how early Protestants reformed the administration of social welfare."[25] Calvin's first major contribution to welfare reform in Geneva is found in his *Ecclesiastical Ordinances* of 1541, what amounts to a constitution for the reforming church in Geneva, in which Calvin, drawing upon his exegesis of the Book of Acts and

21. Ibid.

22. Ibid.

23. Kingdon, "Social Welfare in Calvin's Geneva," 50.

24. Ibid., 51.

25. Ibid., 52.

its description of the early Christian churches, divides church governance into four ministerial offices: (1) pastors who preach the Word of God, (2) doctors who study and teach the Word of God, (3) elders who govern and maintain Christian discipline, and (4) deacons who care for the poor. The latter category, the diaconal ministry, Calvin divides into two distinct categories based on his interpretation of a passage from Paul's letter to the Romans: "Since it is certain that Paul is speaking of the public office of the church, there must have been two distinct grades. Unless my judgment deceive me, in the first clause he designates the deacons who distribute the alms. But the second refers to those who had devoted themselves to the care of the poor and sick" (4.3.9).

The distinctly Calvinist Reformed tradition recognizes plural ministries—both lay and ordained—as necessary for the life of the church because they are so instituted by God. The two fundamental ecclesial offices recognized by Calvin are that of presbyter and deacon. Departing from the Roman Catholic reading of New Testament terminology in which *episkopos* (bishop) and *presbyteros* (priest) are different offices, Calvin argues that according to scriptural usage the various terms for those who govern the church—bishop, presbyter, pastor, and minister—are interchangeable and refer to the same office (4.3.8). According to Calvin, the New Testament identifies only two permanent offices in the church: church governors or elders (*presbyteros*), and those charged with the care of the poor (*diakonos*). Church governance (the ministry of the Word, administration of the sacraments, teaching the faith, and moral guidance and discipline) is thus shared by the clergy, ordained to the ministry of the Word and sacrament, and lay church leaders ("elders chosen from the people") elected to work with the pastors in the day-to-day governance of congregations, especially in resolving conflicts and disciplining believers. The care of the poor (*diakonia*) is further subdivided into two kinds of deacons, those who administer and distribute the alms and those who minister physically to the sick and the poor (4.3.9): "Calvin concludes that the Lukan narrative is more than a story; it is prescriptive for the church order for all time. The office of deacon—the deacon who cares for the poor—is a permanent and a necessary part of organized Christian ministry as love, *caritas*, is as an expression of Christian faith."[26] The end result is an ecclesiology characterized by shared governance rather than autonomous unilateral authority, with an inescapable corporate commitment to the love of neighbor made possible by the

26. McKee, *John Calvin*, 156–57.

Holy Spirit. In historian Elsie McKee's summation, John Calvin defines diaconal ministry as "a permanent ministry of care for the poor and sick, the ministry of the church as a body to the physical suffering of human beings."[27]

The founding of the Geneva General Hospital (*Hôpital-Général*) was part of the Protestant reforms in Geneva initiated before Calvin was invited to preach there. Established by laypersons in 1535 as part of the city's efforts to sever all ties with the Roman Catholic Church, the General Hospital is best described as a general social welfare agency providing "hospitality" to meet a variety of human needs. The hospital housed several dozen orphans and foundlings, as well as people too old or infirm to care for themselves; deacons distributed food on a weekly basis to poor families in the area; and the hospital provided temporary shelter and food to travelers and refugees unable to pay for such accommodations. The administration of the General Hospital was divided between the *procureur*, who served as financial administrator and oversaw the procurement of funds, and the *hospitalliers*, who directed the actual care of the poor. While there is some debate as to how much influence this established—and highly successful—pattern of care shaped Calvin's interpretation of Romans 12:8, with its two-fold diaconate later institutionalized in the 1541 *Ecclesiastical Ordinances*, it is also the case that Calvin's views on the diaconate were formed prior to his arrival in Geneva under the influence of Martin Bucer's teaching on plural ministries. Nevertheless, what develops in Geneva's diaconal ministry is a distinction between those responsible for the judicious fiscal management of poor relief, and those directing and conducting ministries of compassion. This two-fold, permanent ministry of the church allows for the efficient, long-term management of poor relief without detracting from or delaying the church's compassionate response to human suffering.

It is in the context of providing appropriate pastoral response to human needs that the diaconate came to differentiate the care of native Genevans through the General Hospital from care for Geneva's burgeoning refugee population through the French Fund (*Bourse française*). Due to Geneva's geographic limitations—in the sixteenth century it was a modest-size city with a small area of surrounding farmland (converted from existing suburbs after the break with the Roman Catholic Church), besieged by political enemies with standing armies—the city was ill equipped to handle

---

27. McKee, *Diakonia*, 64. For a full discussion of Calvin's understanding of the office of deacon, see McKee, *John Calvin*, chs. 5–9.

such a large influx of political refugees who were competing with native Genevans over very limited resources. Needless to say, this created xeno-phobic sentiments among the native populace (as evidenced by the Perrin revolt of 1555, in which Genevan citizens crowded the streets chanting "kill the French" at the instigation of Ami Perrin), but even the most charitable Genevans hoped most refugees were not planning to settle permanently. The city's General Hospital, used to serving the needs of an estimated 500 impoverished Genevans per annum, could not handle the thousands of refugees streaming into the city. While many of the refugees arriving in Geneva were affluent, as displaced persons all refugees would need cer-tain basic assistance until they were properly settled, not to mention those families who had lost their primary provider (often as the result of political violence, as during the 1544–1545 persecution of evangelicals in southeast-ern France) and came to depend entirely upon the kindness of strangers. To meet the severe social problems caused by immigration, wealthy French refugees established the *Bourse des pauvres étrangers français*, commonly called the French Fund, circa 1545 during this period of intensified per-secution in France, and records indicate that by 1549 the deacons were managing this fund as part of the church's comprehensive poor relief, just prior to the greatest wave of French political and religious immigration.[28]

The French Fund existed primarily to collect money from wealthy refugees, and then responsibly distribute these resources to poor refugees (John Calvin quietly supported the work of the French Fund for years from his own modest income). Eventually, some of these resources were also allocated toward establishing Reformed congregations in France, thereby addressing some of the problems caused by immigration by repatriating French refugees. Apart from emergency relief and medical services, the deacons used this fund to obtain housing for refugee families, or to help refugees secure employment by providing work tools or paying for retrain-ing in order to ensure that refugees did not depend on charity for their long-term subsistence. At its inception, the French Fund provided assis-tance to any who requested and were judged in genuine need, but as the refugee situation worsened, it focused solely on the needs of French im-migrants (by far the largest refugee population). In time, similar funds were established by the various ethnic communities seeking refuge in Geneva and carefully administered by the diaconate. John Calvin's commitment to

28. For the most comprehensive archival study of the activities of the French Fund, see Olson, *Calvin and Social Welfare*.

an ecumenical, international Reformed church underlies this commitment to the social and economic practices of the diaconal ministry in Geneva, but this international scope is also attested by the founding of the Genevan Academy for educating clergy and doctors of the church to serve the nascent Protestant communities of Europe. Accordingly, a certain level of multicultural tolerance and ethnic diversity was intrinsic to Calvin's vision of church order and governance, for while most of these reforms were implemented locally, each local church was viewed as part of "a network of churches, geographically separate, each possessing its own confession . . . a family in which there was room for some diversity in common communion."[29] Consequently, a church wanting to stand within this Calvinist, Reformed tradition ought to demonstrate sensitivity in its corporate life to the needs of immigrants and other displaced persons.

The Christian Life as Sojourn and Exile

Calvinist piety is distinguished by a balancing of spiritual and temporal concerns in its liturgy, governance, and discipline. Social and economic matters do not stand outside theological concerns but are inherently part of the proper worship of God:

> No sixteenth-century persons who followed Calvin's theology would ever be able to separate how they ruled their subjects, nursed their sick neighbors, priced the goods in their shops, or obeyed their parents or disciplined their children from their relationship to God. God always comes first, but the honor owed to God is often most clearly manifested in how believers live their day-to-day vocations.[30]

Care for the refugee and political exile is but one among many possible instantiations of love of neighbor. However, what distinguished Calvin's theology and ethics from many of his contemporaries, is that for Calvin, poor relief is a necessary function of the church embodied in a permanent office, the diaconate.

The church, while independent and distinct from civil authorities, has the "continual responsibility to be actively involved in the social, economic, and educational realities of the world in which it lives,"[31] both in its com-

---

29. McKee, "Character and Significance," 19.

30. Ibid., 21.

31. Ibid., 23.

passionate ministries, and as a voice in the public discourse advocating for a more just state. Underlying this civically engaged corporate piety is a firm theological conviction that "We are not our own. . . . We are God's: let all the parts of our life accordingly strive toward him as our only lawful goal" (3.7.1). In other words, there is no aspect of human life—however mundane—that is not dedicated to God.

John Calvin's theological vision is grounded in the axiom that God is good and just; therefore, whatever God wills is by definition good and just. Calvin's doctrine of providence emphatically affirms that all events in human history are governed by God's secret plan for "nothing happens except what is knowingly and willingly decreed by him" (1.16.3). This understanding of God is not that of a Creator who sits idly by, content to merely observe the creation, but of a participant in every aspect of the natural order and every detail of human culture and history. God truly "governs all events" and "directs everything by his incomprehensible wisdom and disposes it to his own end" (1.16.4). Given this fundamental assumption, belief in a benevolent, guiding providence follows from the knowledge of God received through the power of the Holy Spirit that confirms in our hearts that Jesus Christ is the sole Savior. In Christ, therefore, we can trust that God reigns over all, that evil is under God's providential control, and we are then able to set aside all undue anxiety when confronted by suffering and evil in the world. Hence, Calvin exhorts the believer to display "gratitude of mind for the favorable outcome of things, patience in adversity, and also incredible freedom from worry about the future all necessarily follow from this knowledge [of providence]" (1.17.7). Yet, such forbearance is not passive, but carries with it corresponding social responsibilities.

Even Calvin's strongest critics acknowledge his genuine concern for the suffering of others—not only for those like him who suffered religious persecution—but also for all those who are the innocent victims of injustice:

> I say that not only they who labor for the defense of the gospel but they who in any way maintain the cause of righteousness suffer persecution for righteousness. Therefore, whether in declaring God's truth against Satan's falsehoods or in taking up the protection of the good and the innocent against the wrongs of the wicked, we must undergo the offenses and hatred of the world, which may imperil either our life, our fortunes, or our honor. (3.8.7)

Consequently, Calvin centers spiritual discipline on the practice of self-denial and forbearance for the sake of the neighbor, and characterizes the

Christian life as a response to the grace of God through a life of faithful obedience. In book three of the *Institutes of the Christian Religion*, Calvin delineates four central features of the Christian life: (1) self-denial, (2) bearing the cross, (3) meditation on the future (i.e., heavenly life), and (4) the proper use and enjoyment of this present life. Accordingly, the most adequate image for the Christian is that of a pilgrim or sojourner in this world, whose proper home is the Kingdom of God: "Whatever kind of tribulation presses upon us, we must ever look to this end: to accustom ourselves to contempt for the present life and to be aroused thereby to meditate upon the future life" (3.9.10). That is not to say, however, that we should deny the goodness of God's creation as intended for our well-being, for Calvin also writes, "Away, then, with that inhuman philosophy which, while conceding only a necessary use of creatures, not only malignantly deprives us of the lawful fruit of God's beneficence but cannot be practiced unless it robs a man of all his senses and degrades him" (3.10.3). Yet, this "contempt" for the world is an affirmation that the theme of exile is the most adequate theological framework for understanding human life: "For, if heaven is our homeland, what else is the earth but our place of exile?" (3.9.4).

Following Christ by bearing our cross is possible when we "learn that this life, judged in itself, is troubled, turbulent, unhappy in countless ways, and in no respect clearly happy; that all those things which are judged to be its goods are uncertain, fleeting, vain, and vitiated by many intermingled evils. From this, at the same time, we conclude that in this life we are to seek and hope for nothing but struggle" (3.9.1). It is because of the cross—Christ's sacrifice for us—that we can bear the cross for others. It follows that the right use of God's good gifts is inseparable from our life together in a civil society. For John Calvin, the exploitation and suffering of the poor and powerless is a sinful act—a violation of the image of God all humanity bears (3.7.6)—therefore it is a Christian duty to not only alleviate this suffering through ministries of compassion, but also to order social life in faithfulness to God so as to eliminate suffering.

Conclusion

The "problem" of immigration in the United States is longstanding. While the national narrative contains within it the notion that the United States is a nation of immigrants, "each new wave of immigrants has encountered strenuous opposition from earlier arrivals, who have insisted that the country was already filled to capacity."[32] Since the 1970s, consistent migration from Latin America has altered the face of U.S. demographics, making Latino/as the single largest minority population in the nation. According to the 2010 U.S. Census, the Hispanic population, currently 50.5 million, or 16 percent of the general population, is the fastest growing segment of the population, accounting for more than half of the growth in the total U.S. population between 2000 and 2010. Undocumented immigration from Latin America accounts for much of this growth, as studies on the number of undocumented workers in the U.S. indicate that this segment of the population has grown from an estimated 6 million in 1986, to an estimated 12 million in 2012. Yet, contrary to popular misconceptions, the rapid growth of the Latino/a population since 1990 is not primarily due to illegal immigration, but is attributable to Latino/as having the highest birth rate among all ethnic groups. In fact, 60.9 percent of U.S. Hispanics are native-born, among those who are foreign-born 10 percent are naturalized citizens, and of the remaining new immigrants, almost half entered the country legally. Census data disproves further stereotypes by revealing that the majority (71.8%) of Latino/as who speak Spanish at home are also proficient or fluent in English, and that over 90 percent of second generation Latino/a immigrants list English as their first language, suggesting that as a group Latino/as are no more likely to resist cultural assimilation. Then why the cultural and political backlash targeting undocumented immigration from Latin America?

The Latino/a experience in the United States can be understood in terms of navigating the poles of assimilation and resistance. Latino/as are part of U.S. culture—shaped by it, but also shaping it. They have intermarried, have a long and distinguished history of public service in politics, education, and the military, and have contributed immensely to the religious life of this country. Hispanics now occupy every rung of the socioeconomic ladder, from undocumented farm workers and day laborers to CEOs of large multinational corporations. Yet, despite such inroads into mainstream U.S. culture, Latino/a church communities tend to promote and develop bilingual and bicultural theologies that embody a liberative reading of the Gospel in a society *still* defined in terms of racial, gender, economic, and ethnic inequalities. Therefore, as the presence of Latino/as in the United States continues to grow—and with it the ability to influence and transform society—challenges will inevitably arise to Latino/a

32. Sassen, *Globalization*, 31.

theology's commitment to fulfilling the Biblical imperative to be advocates for the voiceless and powerless who inhabit the margins of society. To that end, Latino/a theologians and ethicists working from within an explicitly liberative framework, informed and guided by this history of marginalization and disenfranchisement, might be surprised to find an ally in John Calvin's theological and exegetical works.

The most contentious immigration debates in the United States have centered on the issues of illegal immigration, border control, and the burden undocumented workers then place on public services. The National Council of La Raza has chronicled on their website (http://www.nclr.org/) many misconceptions about immigration—legal and illegal—that continue to be presented as fact in these debates. One common misconception is that immigrants take jobs away from U.S. citizens. A recent study by the National Federation of Independent Businesses shows that immigrant labor is needed to fill jobs that the older, better educated American workforce is not willing to fill in the areas of agriculture, food processing and production, and the hotel and food service industry. In fact, American small businesses rely on undocumented labor, and are often obstructionists when it comes to comprehensive immigration reform.

As sociologist Saskia Sassen has argued, the "Achilles' heel of U.S. immigration policy has been insistence on viewing immigration as an autonomous process unrelated to other international processes."[33] In other words, U.S. policy makers view the influx of immigrants from the developing world into the United States as primarily caused by limited economic opportunities in the Third World; emigrants leaving undesirable living and working conditions for better economic opportunities elsewhere. However, such simplistic analysis ignores the impact First World economic policies have in the developing world to precipitate and perpetuate the very conditions motivating such migration. Sassen points to the proliferation of "service employment regimes" in the First World as the major contributing factor fueling immigration into the United States, and argues that current efforts to reform immigration policies, "sanctions on employers, deportation of illegal immigrants, stepped-up border patrols—are unlikely to stem the flow" of illegal immigration.[34] In effect, entire industries have created a sense of "general economic insecurity" by shifting away from full-time employment to reliance on temporary workers, thereby forming a new

33. Ibid., 49.
34. Ibid.

underclass increasingly dependent on temporary work that Sassen calls "employment-centered poverty." As less and less of the American workforce pursues these inherently unstable jobs, employers turn to undocumented workers for a renewable source of cheap labor.

Analyzing the morality of immigration reform from the perspective of a Calvinist social ethics, with its emphasis on preserving basic human dignity and establishing a more just state, it is imperative to shift the discussion away from the undocumented worker and onto the business owner. The root cause of illegal immigration is the market demand for an undocumented—and therefore easily exploitable—workforce. In 2009, Giant Labor Solutions and two other Midwestern companies, were indicted under the federal Racketeer Influenced and Corrupt Organizations Act (RICO) for turning their workers into slaves, outsourcing them to housekeeping jobs in hotels and other businesses in 14 different states while forcing them to live, sometimes eight at a time, in small apartments for which these workers were charged exorbitant rent. Most of the workers, primarily from the Dominican Republic, Jamaica, and the Philippines, were in the country illegally and were threatened with deportation and physical harm. This case, and others like it, reveals a pattern of predatory exploitation of undocumented workers by American businesses as a means of not just filling undesirable jobs, but of reducing operating costs for the sole purpose of maximizing profit. Churches standing in the tradition of Calvin, guided by the social welfare reforms implemented in sixteenth-century Geneva, need to respond to those pundits who trample on the basic human rights of undocumented workers because they entered the country illegally, by shifting the focus of the public debate onto the corrupt and oppressive hiring practices of American small business owners.

Supporters of free trade argue that economic globalization has improved wages and working conditions for workers in underdeveloped nations. Detractors contend that the exploitation of weaker nations by the First World has led to an increased wealth gap between developed and underdeveloped nations, has caused unchecked environmental degradation, and when factoring for inflation, has actually resulted in reduced workers' wages. In Latin America, trade liberalization has led to the destruction of jobs and falling real wages, leading to the commodification of human labor to the point that the exportation of human labor (legally or illegally) has become a significant part of many nations' Gross Domestic Product (GDP). In fact, the World Trade Organization includes remittances—the transfer of money by a foreign worker to his/her country of origin—when calculating a nation's GDP since remittances now account for 10 percent or more of the GDP in seven Latin American and Caribbean nations (Guatemala 9.8%, Nicaragua 10.3%, Jamaica 13.8%, Haiti 15.4%, El Salvador 15.7%, Guyana 17.3%, and Honduras 21%). A Reformed theological response to the social problems caused by immigration into the United States cannot ignore these dehumanizing and exploitative policies that perpetuate the flow of undocumented workers into the U.S. solely for the benefit of U.S. businesses. In the spirit of comprehensive welfare reform in Calvin's Geneva, Reformed churches in the U.S. need to articulate a two-fold response by prioritizing ministries of compassion that provide comfort and aid to undocumented workers and the victims of human trafficking, while also advocating for genuine reform of immigration policies grounded in respect for basic human rights. Only then do they remain true to Calvin's conviction "that the Redeemer God is also the Giver of the human society and earthly blessings that human beings enjoy and for which they are accountable."[35] Only then—according to the Calvinist Reformed theological tradition—is God being properly praised.

Discussion Questions

1. What does it say about the culture and mores of our society that the U.S. is one of the world's leading markets for the victims of human trafficking?

2. How ought the Christian doctrine of *imago Dei* impact and guide a discussion of immigration reform?

3. The Calvinist Reformed tradition has a high sense of calling for the office of magistrate, and is comfortable with employing the political process as a means to an end when it comes to creating a more just society. Are there conflicts between Calvin's view of divinely ordained government and his call for Christian political involvement?

4. In many ways, John Calvin's commitment to reforming the church across all of Europe prefigured today's global church with its more ecumenical outlook. What is the relationship of ethnicity and nationality to ecclesial identity?

35. McKee, "Character and Significance," 24.

5. In 2012, the General Assembly of the Presbyterian Church (U.S.A.)—a denomination self-identified as Calvinist and Reformed—approved a statement supporting comprehensive immigration reform.[36] Though John Calvin is never mentioned, are there similarities in approach and content between this statement and John Calvin's outreach to immigrants in sixteenth-century Geneva?

---

36. See http://www.pcusa.org/media/uploads/oga/pdf/ga220-immigration-comprehensive.pdf.

Immigration in the U.S. and Wesleyan Methodology[1]

Hugo Magallanes

ALMOST WITHOUT A DOUBT, everyone reading the pages of this book has an opinion regarding what the U.S. policy on immigration should be and what kind of practices should be adopted and enforced by the government. If this is the case, then why should we read another book or article on this topic? Can this chapter present a new and persuasive argument that would lead readers to a change in their position? Would there be strong convincing evidence and new stories that would persuade readers to change their already informed opinions? My ministerial experience and teaching experience lead me to believe that, for the most part, persons do not change their mind when it comes to controversial issues. For many adults, once they arrive at a conclusion (theological or political) and feel quite comfortable with it, it is difficult for them to change their minds and even more difficult, almost impossible, to embrace the opposing view.

If my experience is right and my pragmatic observation serves as a good indicator, then my questions remain: Why another collection of articles addressing the immigration debate? Furthermore, persons who identify themselves with the Wesleyan/Methodist tradition are no different from the society at large, in the sense that the great majority of them have quite strong informed opinions and believe that their opinions are supported by the Scriptures as well as their Methodist/Wesleyan tradition.

---

1. This essay is based on and a continuation of Magallanes, "Wesleyan Ethics," 833–36.

Again, what would the readers find in here that would make them reconsider their position?

In response to the questions that I believe many readers would ask, I begin this essay by stating that it is not my goal to reverse the reader's position on the immigration debate, nor is it my desire to persuade readers to change their mind, although this may occur as a result of what I am about to propose here. My primary goal in this chapter is to explore and analyze the approach that was employed by those who have arrived at a conclusion on the immigration debate. In other words, I do not want to argue about what position is right or who is wrong, but rather I want to invite those who are in favor of and against immigration reform, those who have arrived at a conclusion regarding immigration in the U.S., and everyone in between to consider the methodology employed in arriving at their respective conclusions. I truly believe that methodologies and discussions about them are much more important than arguing who is right or wrong based on conclusions alone.

I have discovered that many persons who have very strong opinions on certain issues very seldom are able to articulate how their theological and Christian tradition assisted them in arriving at their conclusions. Quite often these persons simply embrace and replicate political positions, which are common and acceptable in their context, without having the opportunity to explore and analyze the implications of their conclusions from a theological perspective and without considering the theological method employed to reach these conclusions.[2] Therefore in this chapter, I intend to offer suggestions as to what elements and aspects would be important to consider in our methodologies, of course from a Methodist/Wesleyan perspective, as we ponder how we reached our conclusions in the heated immigration debate.

---

2. Perhaps an example of this is the argument presented to support a pro-life position, in which those who embrace this position are also in favor of capital punishment. In my opinion this seems contradictory. If the argument for pro-life is grounded on the premise that life is sacred and therefore should be preserved, then why is it justifiable to take the life of a person who has been found guilty of a crime? Again, I do not want to take a position here, but simply highlight the importance of the method and implications of the argument, and how these should be consistent with other moral issues and dilemmas.

John Wesley's Methodology:
A Brief Overview

What does an Anglican Priest, who lived in eighteenth-century England, who believed in the divine rights of the monarchy, and who did not support the independence of the Thirteen Colonies, have to say about immigrants and immigration policies in the U.S. in the second decade of the 21st century? In response to this question, some would affirm categorically that he has nothing to offer or say. He simply cannot; he is not present with us. Any attempts to offer a Wesleyan perspective on this issue would be pure speculation. Others would propose that even though Wesley is obviously no longer with us, those who identify him as the founder of the Methodist/ Wesleyan movement would argue that there are certain aspects that are characteristic and intrinsic to the movement, and that these would provide a Wesleyan perspective to the immigration debate. I tend to agree more with the latter position. I believe that there are aspects that are central to the Wesleyan/Methodist identity, but these aspects are not a set of rules or traditions. In my opinion, the distinctive aspect in the Wesleyan/Methodist tradition is its methodology.[3] Thus, if the Wesleyan methodology is applied and followed in addressing particular situations, such as immigration, then the response would carry essential Methodist characteristics. For this reason, I would like to suggest an exploration of Wesley's methodology first and then use it to address the immigration dilemmas before us.

In attempting to discern Wesley's methodology one is required to explore Wesley's life, his ministerial work, and his writings to determine the underlying steps and approach as well as their consistency.[4] To start with his personal life, whoever is somewhat familiar with John Wesley's life would know that he had a dramatic change, a personal conversion, and change of mind. Wesley himself makes reference to this experience as a key moment in his life and identified it as a turning point. I am referring to his "Aldersgate experience," which is perhaps the most remarkable event of his life. Wesley described it as follows:

---

3. Others have identified methodologies in approaches to Wesleyan Theology. See: Outler, "Wesleyan Quadrilateral," 7–18; and Gunter et al., *Wesley and the Quadrilateral.*

4. Several authors, who follow this approach, include: Chilcote, *Recapturing the Wesleys' Vision*; Harper, *Way to Heaven*; Snyder, *Radical Wesley*; Maddox, ed., *Responsible Grace*; Hynson, *To Reform the Nation*; and Thorsen, *Wesleyan Quadrilateral.*

> . . . I felt my heart strangely warmed. I felt I did trust in Christ, Christ alone for salvation: And an assurance was given me, that he had taken away my sins, even mine, and saved me from the law of sin and death. I began to pray with all my might for those who had in a more especial manner despitefully used me and persecuted me. I then testified openly to all there, what I now first felt in my heart.[5]

Wesley's well known account of his experience at Aldersgate shows that there was a paradigm shift in his belief system,[6] which, at the "spiritual" level, led him to place his trust in Christ alone and to reach a point of certainty regarding Christ's work in terms of deliverance from the law of sin and death. It is important to note that, in addition to the heavy-loaded theological language employed by Wesley, he highlights and employs the language of deliverance and its connection to the legal motif, "saved from the law of sin and death." This is a crucial aspect that needs to be considered in exploring Wesley's methodological approach. The importance of this significant shift is highlighted by Wesley's own account, in which he seems to indicate that before Aldersgate, he was following a legal approach and methodology. In other words, in this statement he implies that before Aldersgate he felt obligated to fulfill his Christian duty. Thus his methodology could be labeled as deontological. If this is true, then Wesley's primary reasons for his actions and even his ministerial work were grounded in a sense of duty and legal obligation.

After Aldersgate Wesley seems to have changed his approach.[7] He is now moved by God's love, no longer bound to a legalistic and deontological approach. In fact, in his initial account of his experience there is a clear indication of this shift. As his first action Wesley prayed for those who "despitefully used" him and "persecuted" him. In considering Wesley's words and his personal testimony, I wonder: Did Wesley not pray for his enemies before this occasion? If he did, what was he asking God to do with them? Perhaps in his strict legalistic sense and following his duty, Wesley asked God to punish them. Maybe Wesley asked God to lead them to repentance; or maybe Wesley did not feel compelled to pray for his enemies at all. After his personal transformation, however, Wesley seems to develop a sense of

5. Wesley, *Works of John Wesley*, 1:103.

6. For an overview of multiple interpretations of this event, see Collins, "Twentieth-Century Interpretations," 18–31.

7. For an excellent description of this "paradigm shift," see Lovin, "Moral Theology," 647–61.

moral responsibility for his enemies and those who "used" him. Of course, not out of a deontological imposition but rather in response to God's work in his life. God accepted him, welcomed him, and gave him peace in his heart, while he had considered himself an enemy of God! Now, as a response to God's love and embrace, Wesley wants to do the same for all people, including praying for his enemies and publicly testifying of these actions.

It is evident that at Aldersgate Wesley experienced a methodological shift as well as a personal transformative moment, in which Wesley was moved by God's love, to love others in an attempt to replicate God's character and acceptance that God demonstrated to him. And for this reason, his methodology is precisely grounded in trying to replicate God's love and character, which can be described in Christian ethics as character or virtue ethics. Furthermore, his ministerial work and his writings seem to corroborate this fundamental shift in his methodological approach. For example, before Aldersgate Wesley practiced personal spiritual disciplines and became quite active in social work, but reflecting on these years at Oxford as a member of the Holy Club, Wesley wrote:

> More especially, we call upon those who for many years saw our manner of life at Oxford. These well know that "after the straitest sect of our religion we lived [like] Pharisees;" and that the grand objection to us for all those years was, the being righteous overmuch; the reading, fasting, praying, denying ourselves,—the going to church, and to the Lord's table,—the relieving the poor, visiting those that were sick and in prison, instructing the ignorant, and labouring to reclaim the wicked,—more than was necessary for salvation. These were our open, flagrant crimes, from the year 1729 to the year 1737.[8]

Therefore, and by his own admission, his work during the Oxford years reflected a legalistic (Pharisaical) and deontological tendency as his ethical and moral impulse, which reiterates the methodological shift and the striking contrast in his life and ministry after Aldersgate.

Wesley's emphasis on reflecting God's character is not only the basis for his personal morality and his methodological approach, but Wesley takes this approach to critique the philosophers of his time. He stated in one of his sermons:

> But how great is the number of those who, allowing religion to consist of two branches,—our duty to God, and our duty to our

8. Wesley, *Works of John Wesley*, 8:29.

neighbour,—entirely forget the first part, and put the second part for the whole,—for the entire duty of man! Thus almost all men of letters, both in England, France, Germany, yea, and all the civilized countries of Europe, extol humanity to the skies, as the very essence of religion. To this the great triumvirate, Rousseau, Voltaire, and David Hume, have contributed all their labours, sparing no pains to establish a religion which should stand on its own foundation, independent on any revelation whatever; yea, not supposing even the being of a God. So leaving Him, if he has any being, to himself, they have found out both a religion and a happiness which have no relation at all to God, nor any dependence upon him. It is no wonder that this religion should grow fashionable, and spread far and wide in the world. But call it humanity, virtue, morality, or what you please, it is neither better nor worse than Atheism. Men hereby wilfully and designedly put asunder what God has joined,—the duties of the first and the second table. It is separating the love of our neighbour from the love of God.[9]

In this paragraph, although Wesley uses deontological language, he offers a critique of humanistic ethical and philosophical methods, which promote an anthropocentric view of life, and places value in being "good" to others for their sake. For Wesley, though, this approach is flawed, because it ignores God as the main source of love and goodness and God's nature and character, which is centered in the importance of relationships—with God and with one another, of course including enemies as well. Wesley's emphasis on relationships and God as the ultimate source of love provide the core of his ethical and methodological approach.

After this initial analysis of Wesley's methodological approach and his dramatic change, it is important for us to consider our own approach and how closely connected it is to Wesley's approach as we deal with the immigration dilemma. For example, do we subscribe to a deontological approach, in which the most important aspect in our moral reasoning is to obey the law and follow our duty out of a sense of obligation? Or, do we try to reflect God's character and God's unconditional love in every aspect of our life, even when dealing with moral dilemmas? Obviously these two questions point to Wesley's methodology before and after his experience in Aldersgate, and each approach would lead us to different decisions. If we place a high value on obedience to the law as our moral duty, then our answer to the immigration debate would be somewhat easy to resolve: obey

9. Wesley, *Works of John Wesley*, 7:270–71.

the law and compel others to do so. Now, if we believe that obedience to the law is the ultimate moral virtue, then some may be persuaded to follow this approach, which is helpful in some instances. However, in some cases, the effectiveness and morality of it is questioned. Due to space and time limitations, I am not able to elaborate on this position, but I would like to provide an example of the moral shortcomings of this deontological approach.[10]

In the U.S. and many other countries slavery was a legal practice, and in this country a practice and system that was kept in place for more than three hundred years. During these years, the main arguments used to sustain such an oppressive system were grounded in legal, biological, and economic aspects. Thus, many who subscribed to unconditional obedience to the law of the land had a very difficult time in embracing positions and arguments in favor of abolition, since slavery was a lawful and well-accepted practice. Even after slavery was banned, many believed that changing this law was a mistake. For this and other reasons, I would like to suggest that following the law, using a deontological approach as the only moral compass to explore personal and social dilemmas, may not be the best way to resolve and address moral dilemmas. Furthermore, as I presented above, Wesley followed this method in his personal Christian journey and found it to be less than ideal in his pursuit of holiness.

Taking into consideration Wesley's immediate reaction as presented in his recollection of his Aldersgate experience—that is, that he prayed for his enemies—and connecting this action to other ministerial approaches he embraced as well as additional notes in his journal, it is evident that Wesley's main desire was to demonstrate God's love to all, not only to people like him, not only to those with similar ideas, but also to his enemies. Wesley's approach is not just a sentence in his testimony; it was a lifelong desire to love others and to do so the same way that God had loved him. Returning to the slavery system in the U.S.: Wesley was exposed to it while serving as a missionary in Georgia before his Aldersgate experience. Wesley, following a deontological and legalistic approach to this issue, did not challenge the evils of slavery, but as a pastor wondered about the well being of the souls of slaves. While he had the opportunity to question and oppose the slavery system in Georgia, he did not. However, years later, after Aldersgate, and following his new methodology, he embraced the abolitionist position.[11]

10. For an overview of the difficulties in using this approach, see Ogletree, *Use of the Bible*, 1–46.

11. For an explanation of Wesley's theological journey with respect to slavery, see

Perhaps we will be better equipped if we take Wesley's methodological approach, after his Aldersgate experience, as our daily practice. If this is the case, then our questions should not only be based on what is legal or what is our duty. Rather we should ask ourselves, How would beginning from God's character and love lead us to respond to the moral challenges we face? What might God say about treating strangers and foreigners in our land? Who is included or excluded in God's definition of neighbor? Did the main characters in the Old and New Testament follow the law of the land? Were they compelled to break the law for the sake of protecting the innocent, the vulnerable, the poor, and those marginalized by society?[12] I consider these questions very helpful as we consider the type of method and approach we use from a theological perspective for moral dilemmas such as immigration. I, like John Wesley's account of his experience at Aldersgate, believe that reflecting God's character and reflecting God's love is the best way to approach this and other dilemmas. I would like to suggest that in order to do so, the following key elements in Wesley's theology are instrumental in assisting us in our moral reasoning and methodological approach.

Key Elements in Wesley's Methodology and Approach

Although reflecting God's love and demonstrating love for the neighbor are general themes in John Wesley's sermons and his journal entries, a detailed look at these general themes helps us to easily identify unique elements, which in turn provide essential and instrumental aspects for Wesley's ethical and theological approach. Such elements include: the image of God in humans, salvation, and the importance of free will. I will explore each of these elements, and then I will explain how these aspects may help us as we consider them in our own methodology.

The image of God, according to Wesley, is central for understanding salvation and the human condition after the fall of humanity. Wesley uses the creation story and the image of God to highlight the state of perfection and the harmony present between the Creator and all created beings.

Carey, "Wesley's *Thoughts upon Slavery*," 269–84; and Walker, "Wesley as Abolitionist," 26–27.

12. In responding to these questions, it would be important to read and consider the story of the birth of Moses and how he was saved at birth, and the story of Rahab and how she saved the Israelite spies.

The image of God, for Wesley, provides the moral framework of reference for our Christian life, since it is intrinsically connected to the moment of creation and later to our salvation. Evidence of this is found in Wesley's sermon "The New Birth," in which he affirms:

> Why must we be born again? What is the foundation of this doctrine? The foundation of it lies near as deep as the creation of the world; in the scriptural account whereof we read, "And God," the three-one God, "said, Let us make man in our image, after our likeness. So God created man in his own image, in the image of God created he him." Not barely in his natural image, a picture of his own immortality; a spiritual being, endued with understanding, freedom of will, and various affections; nor merely in his political image, the governor of this lower world, having "dominion over the fishes of the sea, and over all the earth;" but chiefly in his moral image; which, according to the Apostle, is "righteousness and true holiness." In this image of God was man made. "God is love": Accordingly, man at his creation was full of love; which was the sole principle of all his tempers, thoughts, words, and actions. God is full of justice, mercy, and truth; so was man as he came from the hands of his Creator. God is spotless purity; and so man was in the beginning pure from every sinful blot.[13]

For Wesley, the original state of creation depicts God's character in relationship to the universe and particularly to humans. In this depiction, according to Wesley, God offers a clear picture of what perfection and harmony look like in the "original state." At the same time, this depiction provides a glimpse of the ultimate goal of the Christian life—the return, as much as possible, to this original state after the fall of humanity. In other words, in the creation narrative God established a state of perfect harmony that later is marred by the misuse (and abuse) of human free will, which results in the fall of all of humanity. However, the narrative does not end with a pessimistic tone, where everything and everyone is lost. After the fall of humanity, God sets the ultimate goal for the Christian community, which is precisely the restoration of the original state through the work of Christ, both at the personal and social level. In this way, Wesley argues that the goal of salvation (and holiness) is the restoration of the perfect and harmonious state, thus delineating the moral character of those who consider themselves members of the redeemed community. That is, they are to attempt to reflect and recover this state to the best of their ability and rely on God's grace,

---

13. Wesley, *Works of John Wesley*, 6:66.

particularly as it relates to "the moral image of God," which is, according to Wesley, fulfilled in loving God and neighbor. Love for God and neighbor requires human action, intentionality, and a willingness to do so. It is not something that occurs by divine imposition. Rather, loving God and loving our neighbors implies the use of human free will, using it to reflect God's love and moral character.

Following Wesley's interpretation, God's image and the freedom of choice given to humans provide the essential elements that make humans morally accountable for their actions, since we have a God-given capacity to choose between working toward the restoration and return to the original state or to follow our fallen desires that lead to destruction. The image of God present in every single individual provides moral attributes and the capacity to discern between these choices. Wesley affirms that God is the author of this work, but he also affirms that it requires human participation in the form of a moral choice. At the same time that Wesley and his understanding of the image of God makes humans morally responsible for their choices, it also makes them valuable and worthy of dignity and respect. If all humans have the imprinted image of God, then there is something intrinsically and morally good in them. If God sees value in each of them, then in our deliberations and actions we should show the same kind of appreciation, respect, and protect the dignity of all human beings, due to their God-given condition. Following Wesley's methodological approach, one should be able to affirm that all human beings have the potential to be saved, and those who already are have the additional moral responsibility; to love in the same way God does.

Christians are called and moved by God's grace to follow and reflect God's character in demonstrating God's love. They are not only to accept God's love in a personal way; they also are to apply the same redemptive love toward others and in doing so look for ways to alleviate the social conditions of those who are in need. This instrumental aspect in the Christian journey implies that proactive and intentional steps should be taken to enter in a relationship with all other humans and creatures, as it was reflected in the original state. Thus, Wesleyan methodology is not only a theoretical approach in discerning moral dilemmas. It is also a bold challenge to Christians, calling us to live a life that reflects God's character in community for the well being of the community at large, to always strive to move toward the state of perfection depicted in the creation narrative.

Wesleyan Methodology and the Immigration Debate in the U.S.

As I am writing this essay, there are many candidates running for local and state public office positions in Texas and other states. In many of the television announcements paid for by their campaigns to promote their agendas, these candidates highlight their Christian faith as an important factor in their political career, their decision-making process, and their personal journey. Interestingly enough, in these paid advertisements/announcements, these same candidates also clearly state that they are against "illegal immigration" and that they will not approve in-state tuition for "illegal students." Some will go as far as to say that they will oppose sanctuary cities, since these harbor "illegal immigrants." The position of these candidates is clear: amnesty and extending rights to "illegal immigrants" is absolutely wrong. Others may be willing to entertain a compromise, but this must include a punishment of some sort, since these persons have broken the law and should pay a penalty.

As I said at the beginning, I do not want to change a person's opinion, certainly not the ones of those who have spent thousands of dollars in making public their position on immigration and dealing with "illegal" immigrants. However, in listening to these candidates and other Christians make statements like these, I am very interested to know what is their methodological approach in reaching these strong anti-immigrant positions. How do these self-proclaimed Christians arrive at these conclusions? Did they consider the biblical narrative as a whole or do they pick and select certain passages? Do they perceive any inconsistencies between making a public confession of their faith in Christ and their strong position to eliminate education and health care benefits to those whom they labeled "illegal immigrants"? Are these "illegal immigrants" excluded from having the "image of God" imprinted in them? Do they think that the law of the land, in this case the United States of America, is a clear and perfect reflection of God's law and will?

Of course, I may never get answers to these questions from political candidates, but these and many other questions should be considered by those who call themselves Christian, regardless of whether they are running for office or not. In my opinion, responding to these questions and many others, which are intended to analyze our methodological approach, is of utmost importance, even more important than the conclusion itself.

The conclusion only expresses the final product, but it does not demonstrate the method employed in reaching such a conclusion. For this reason and after briefly considering Wesley's methodology and its key elements, I would like to turn my attention to practical ways in which his approach may be employed in the current debate.

Following Wesley's journey and approach, let us begin by asking ourselves certain simple questions that may shed some light on our ethical system and method: Why are you a Christian? Why do you go to church? If the answer to these questions has to do with faithful obedience to God's law and a sense of assuming these responsibilities out of Christian duty, then persons who respond in this way may be characterized as Wesley before Aldersgate—that is, as living the Christian life in which following laws, rituals, and traditions is a moral imperative. Therefore, their methodological approach will be based on obedience to laws, both Scriptural and governmental. On the other hand, if answers to the above questions are defined in terms of responding to God's love, in being moved by God's unconditional love and mercy and following these practices not as a legal imposition or duty, but rather out of gratitude for the love that was demonstrated to us by God through Christ, then these persons may be classified as the post-Aldersgate Wesley—that is, as persons who are moved by God's infinite and unconditional love and who want to replicate and demonstrate this kind of love in their daily life.

In my opinion, when responding to ethical and moral dilemmas, such as immigration and any other social or personal situations, one should begin with an introspective look at one's motivations and moral compass, particularly as they deal with matters of faith and spiritual disciplines. So, I would suggest that our first step in responding to the immigration debate is to take a critical look at the way we see and understand our own Christian life, vocation, and service to God and others. We should explore the reasons and motivations for our love of God, discern how this love translates into love for our neighbors—fellow human beings created in the image of God—and reflect on who fits and does not fit this category in our minds. In taking this introspective look, it is very important to consider our denominational affiliation and the way our tradition influences our moral reasoning, in the same way we have done in considering Wesley's methodological approach.

Once a general approach has been identified, then I would suggest following and using the three key elements I have highlighted as integral to Wesley's approach. These are: the image of God in humans, salvation, and the importance of free will. If we are in agreement with Wesley and believe that every single human being, regardless of legal status or social and spiritual condition, was created in the image of God, then we must ask ourselves: What is my moral responsibility with regard to so-called "illegal aliens/immigrants," who were created by God and are in God's image? Are they worthy of dignity and respect because God's image is present in their lives? Even if we regard them as persons who have broken the law, does this social transgression eradicate God's image in them?

Before attending to specific matters related to the importance of asserting the image of God in this particular group of persons, let us pause for a moment and think of the person, who may be considered the most evil of all, perhaps an enemy of humanity, perhaps a person who has committed a senseless act, has no regard for others, and intentionally oppresses or abuses others. Was such a person, this perpetrator of horrendous acts, created in the image of God? Does this person, somehow, someway, still carry a glimpse of God's image? Does God love this person? Would God extend unmerited forgiveness and offer mercy and grace to redeem and change the immoral lifestyle embraced by this person? Or, would God simply reject this person because of his/her disobedience? Would God say there is no more grace and forgiveness since he/she had reached some sort of limit? Those of us, who identify with the Wesleyan tradition, will lean toward an inclusive understanding of God's universal grace and affirm the presence of God's image in all persons, including those who are morally pernicious. This understanding and approach challenge us to see every person, regardless of their moral condition, through the lens of God's love, mercy, and kindness—that is, to look for God's image in them, rather than pointing out their multiple moral flaws.

Furthermore, if God's image is present in the cruelest of persons and we are called and challenged to treat these persons with respect and dignity, then what should we do regarding those who are in this country without proper documents, those so-called "illegal immigrants"? If, as Methodists/ Wesleyans, we are called to see the image of God in the worst of persons, then what should our attitude be toward those who are "illegally" in this country? Should we look for ways to ensure their-well being, or should we find ways to enforce the law of the land, when doing so would place many of them in harm's way? What about those who were children when they arrived in this country and whose presence here was not a voluntary decision, since their parents made that choice and took the risk of migrating to this country without proper documents? What about those who are under-age, many of them infants, who were born in this country and enjoy full citizenship? Should their parents be deported because they are not "legal" residents? Who will take care of these underage children and infants? The state? The church?

Perhaps these questions, considered in light of the image of God in every individual, may lead us to the next practical step in our methodology. I would suggest that in this next step one should take a careful look at the way we see and define ourselves and the way we see and define others. Here it would be particularly helpful to remember Wesley's reaction after Aldersgate, when he began to pray for those "who despitefully used me and persecuted me." His reaction can be a good model and pattern for us to follow in considering some of the strong economic arguments used against generous immigration reform policies. Often these arguments are based on financial projections as well as the distribution of limited resources. The main point is that a generous immigration reform would create economic chaos, since many of these immigrants would become a "public charge," who would drain the limited resources available to the law-abiding citizens of this country. Although I find these arguments questionable, instead of citing others who believe that the opposite would be true—that is, that new immigrants would bring economic vitality to the U.S. economy—I would rather focus on the theological method evident in Wesley's reaction after Aldersgate to address these concerns. In this way, even if some are convinced that this new wave of immigrants is taking advantage of the welfare system, and even if the affirmation that their only motivation for risking their lives to come to the U.S. is to enjoy a "free ride" is true, then it is here that remembering Wesley would be an important methodological factor. Let us remember the words employed by Wesley himself, who prayed for those who "despitefully used me."

Furthermore, let us remember the words and example of Christ, who clearly identifies himself with the poor, the homeless, the thirsty, the prisoner,[14] and perhaps in a contextualized way, with the "illegal immigrant," and who also was "used" by others. For example, we should recall the ingratitude of the crowd who picked Barabbas, despite the fact that they were the beneficiaries of Jesus' miracles and kindness, and the words he spoke addressing those who were mocking him while he was hanging from the cross, pronouncing forgiveness and mercy while enduring evil and

14. See Matt 25.

injustice.[15] If Christ and Wesley were able to demonstrate love and forgiveness even to those who mistreated them, then what should characterize our treatment of "illegal immigrants," even when some of us are convinced that they are abusing the system? Do we see the image of God in them? If we do, what is our moral responsibility for those who carry God's image but do not carry a proper documentation?

The next step in our methodology will incorporate two other key theological aspects, namely, salvation and free will. If salvation is seen as the redemption of our current circumstances to reflect those which were described in the creation narrative, before the fall of humanity, and if free will means the capacity to make decisions within certain parameters, then those who consider themselves saved will, in a distinctive and characteristic way, intentionally attempt to reflect the harmony and perfection depicted before the fall. In Genesis 1–2, a perfect balance existed between creatures and creation. There were perfect relationships, in which true dialogue among equals was the norm. Without a doubt, this state of perfection has been lost. However, for the community of Christian believers, restoration is possible, and it is this restoration aspect that becomes crucial in the immigration debate.

In my experience, the great majority of persons who uphold strong positions against immigration reform and policies that favor "illegal" immigrants never have had a conversation and much less a personal relationship with a so-called "illegal immigrant." I find this troublesome in many ways, but even more so, when these persons also uphold strong Christian values. How can they/we say that they/we are Christians, who love God and love our neighbor, but never have had a conversation and/or a personal relationship with an undocumented person? How can they/we affirm that God's image is imprinted in every individual, yet avoid personal contact and conversation with those who lack certain documents? How can they/we say that they/we are working on intentionally restoring broken relationships, when they/we intentionally shun those who are considered lawbreakers? Perhaps this last step would be the most valuable, beneficial, and practical of all, in that it challenges us to have a personal relationship with those very persons who would be adversely affected by (or would benefit from) the immigration policies we propose. By moving in this direction, I would guess that the immigration debate would no longer focus on more abstract socioeconomic or legal issues, but rather on real persons with names and

15. See Matt 27:15–25 and Luke 23:34.

stories, persons whose lives are a product of a complex environment and not a simple statistic with the pejorative label "illegal."

Conclusion

As I stated at the beginning, my goal is not to reverse the position that the great majority of persons already may have when it comes to the immigration debate. Rather I want to invite all of us, who for guidance look to God, the Scriptures, the life and ministry of Christ, and in particular those of us who subscribe to the Methodist/Wesleyan tradition, to also consider John Wesley. He can help us to be self-critical and analytical of the methodology employed in reaching our conclusions and also to recognize the implications not only of our conclusions but also of the method employed. It is my hope that, by returning to Wesley and appreciating the importance of using a theological method to respond to the immigration dilemmas, many of us would be able to explore the steps I have listed here.

Even more than an exploration, I hope and pray that all of us would be moved to talk, relate, and develop personal and communal relationships with those whom we often argue, whether in favor of or against the presence of undocumented immigrants in this country. As Christians, the very least we can do is to engage at a personal level those who are at the center of such heated debates. May God lead us in our decisions, after these conversations and relationships have been formed and developed. Instead of arguing who is right or who is wrong in the immigration debate, I would simply conclude by asking, when was the last time that each one of us had a meaningful conversation with an undocumented person?

Questions for Reflection

1. What is your initial response when you are faced with ethical dilemmas? What sources, traditions, hymns/songs, or scriptural references come to mind? Consider these and think and reflect on your methodological approach.

2. Once you reach a conclusion on a particular topic, how do you treat/regard persons who subscribe and affirm the opposite position?

3. Consider the life and ministry of Christ. Do you think that some people took advantage of him, that is, that some followed him for the "assistance" he offered? If this is the case, how did he treat those who "took advantage" of him?

4. If the main reason undocumented immigrants are here is to take advantage of the U.S. welfare system, what should Christian congregations do in addressing this situation?

5. In many cases, Christians have challenged the U.S. law in order to protect the rights of the marginalized, such as slaves. Why were they persuaded to do so? What led them to "civil disobedience"? Does the current immigration debate warrant a similar response? Why or why not?

————— 5 —————

Pentecostal Politics or Power

Theological Models for Advancing Immigration Reform

Sammy G. Alfaro

Introduction

ON APRIL 23, 2010 when Governor Jan Brewer signed Senate Bill 1070 into law, the Latino community of Arizona braced itself for a political battle with the state and its legislative body, which have since then been at the forefront of the national debate on immigration reform.[1] Over the past couple of years, in which Maricopa County Sherriff Joe Arpaio has sought to implement this law with its full force, Latino/a pastors have seen and felt the first-hand effects of racial profiling, including imprisoned or deported parents, scattered families, a drop in church membership and attendance, and a high increase in unemployment rates among parishioners.[2] As a district pastor overseeing five Pentecostal Church of God (Cleveland, TN) congregations in the Phoenix metropolitan area, I can testify that on average our churches lost 20–30 percent of their parishioners when families

1. For a foundational study of the recent struggle for immigration reform in Arizona, see Espinosa, "'Salvation and Transformation,'" 133–51.

2. Reflecting on the situation Latino churches are facing in Arizona, Gary Kinnaman (a pastor interested in building networks among Latino pastors) writes: "Since the passage of Arizona SB1070, attendance in Spanish language churches in Arizona has dropped by 50%. Families have left our state or stay home on Sundays because the fear of deportation. Most tragically, many families have been ripped apart by deportation." "Ready4Reform," http://ready4reform.org/post/67385357260/gary-as-we-sit-on-our-political-hands-more-people.

migrated away from Arizona after the enactment of SB 1070, seeking work and a less hostile situation for their loved ones.[3]

In the middle of this turmoil, Rev. Steve Montenegro rode the SB 1070 bandwagon and got reelected to a second term as an Arizona State Representative. Yet, much to the chagrin of Latino voters, Montenegro was not reelected on account of his renunciation of SB 1070. On the contrary, he was the only Latino elected official in Arizona who voted in its favor.[4] Montenegro's surname alone is enough to cause a scandal among the Latino community. After all, how could a Latino politician vote in favor of a law that would potentially endanger the well-being of fellow Latinos and their families? To add insult to injury, Montenegro is a faithful member of a local Latino Pentecostal congregation, The Apostolic Assembly of Faith in Surprise, AZ. Even more outrageous, Montenegro's family was sponsored by the Apostolic Assembly as they processed their immigration status from El Salvador in the eighties.[5] So, what would drive a Salvadoran immigrant and minister of the Gospel to side with a bill that the Latino community views as anti-immigration and anti-Latino?

Looking at Rep./Rev. Steve Montenegro as a test case for what happens when Pentecostal power is trumped by political power, this chapter presents a pastoral response, which seeks to establish the foundation for biblically informed and ethically responsible theological models for advancing

3. In a recent study by the Director of the Center for Latino Studies at the Pentecostal Theological Seminary in Cleveland, TN (the flagship seminary of the Church of God), Wilfredo Estrada Adorno declares: "Most of our churches in [the Southeastern] region had a proportion of about 65% to 35% of undocumented to documented members. In some churches that proportion is even higher and still in some others all the members, including the pastor, are undocumented." This declaration points to the struggle of Pentecostal congregations, which tend to attract immigrant families throughout the U.S. Adorno, "Wesleyan Pentecostal Theological Reflection."

4. Shortly after his reelection, Anthea Butler documents Montenegro's political antics like this: "The only Hispanic to vote for SB 1070 is Arizona State Representative Rev. Steve B. Montenegro, a minister in the Apostolic Assembly church—a Oneness Pentecostal denomination with a large Mexican and Mexican-American population. Montenegro, an El Salvadorian immigrant, fled to America with his parents and was granted religious asylum status enabling him to become a citizen. His parents were assisted in that process by obtaining papers from Apostolic Assembly." Butler, "Arizona Is the Hispanic Alabama."

5. A popular blog maintained by Chicano activists in Arizona, *Three Sonorans Blog*, documents the details of Montenegro's immigration story, church involvement, and his turncoat antics by labeling him as *El Vendido* (the "Sell Out"), "Who Is Steve Montenegro?" *Three Sonorans News & Analysis*, July 14, 2010, https://threesonorans.com/2010/07/14/who-is-steve-montenegro-video/.

immigration reform from a Pentecostal perspective. As an implicated Latino pastor and theologian who resides in Phoenix, this political scenario
leads me to ask questions that I believe the Latino community desires to
know concerning the political position of the Latino Pentecostal church.
The leading questions are: (1) Given the number of undocumented immigrants who are members in Latino Pentecostal churches, has the Latino
Pentecostal church been proactive or passive in its response to the plight
of the undocumented parishioners? (2) What can the Latino Pentecostal
church do to actively participate in the fight for immigration reform on
a state and national level? Thus, in preparation for this essay, I had conversations with Latino Pentecostal pastors, leaders, and church attendees
in order to understand the problem from within and to voice the plight
of the undocumented. In addition, I have sought to understand the opposing viewpoint represented by some U.S.-born Latinos who surprisingly
favor SB 1070.[6]

In Search of Pentecostal Voices

There are approximately over 12 million undocumented immigrants in the
U.S. who eagerly await governmental action concerning immigration reform. During this present hopeful interval, Latino/a Catholic and mainline
Protestant scholars and activists have provided solid biblical, ethical, and
theological responses from their respective traditions.[7] While these books
represent a rich portrayal of the current scholarly responses to the social
and ethical problems posed by unjust immigration laws from biblical and

6. An article in the National Public Radio website argues that about 12% of second
generation Latinos living in Arizona fully support SB 1070. O'Dowd, "Some Latinos Support Arizona's New Immigration Law," para. 2

7. For example, consider four of the most recent books on immigration from a
Latino/a or Latino-friendly perspective. Two books, which together provide a good
introduction to biblical, theological, and ethical responses to the critical questions surrounding the immigration debates from Evangelical and Latino Catholic perspectives,
respectively, are: Carroll R., *Christians at the Border*; and Groody and Campese, eds.
A Promised Land. A second pair of books that provide more focused attention to the
voices of the undocumented are: De La Torre, *Trails of Hope and Terror*, which recov-
ers stimulating testimonies on the typical issues of struggle from an ethnically and reli-
giously diverse perspective while weaving a variety of biblical and ethical responses, and
Conde-Frazier, *Listen to the Children/Escuchemos a los niños*, which delivers a moving
tale through conversations on how the children of immigrant and undocumented families are affected by the decision, process, and struggle of immigrating to the U.S.

theological forays, there is an untapped well of reflection that needs to be assessed and brought into the greater theological conversation. Although a great number of undocumented Latinas/os attend Pentecostal churches, the theological reflection and participation focused on the social problems of immigration affecting these congregations has not been a topic for scholarly production specifically from within this religious tradition. In part, this is due to the nature of Pentecostal theology, which historically has focused less on published works and has developed more during church services through the testimonies of the congregation and teaching/preaching of the pastors.[8] Moreover, Latino/a pastors have been occupied in the task of counseling and comforting those dealing with the effects of arrests and deportations within their congregations.

In light of this, there is a great need to survey the work and reflections of Latino/a Pentecostal pastors with the aim of voicing their biblical and theological response to the current debates on immigration reform. Just because there is a lack of published theological writings on immigration from a Latina/o Pentecostal perspective, it does not follow that the Pentecostal community has not been thinking deeply about the political, social, and biblical implications surrounding the issue of immigration reform. The starting point for developing a theology of immigration grounded in the experience of the Latino Pentecostal community is the cry of Spirit-led people who look to God for help believing in divine intervention as a solution for their undocumented status. Whatever is done at the social-political activist level is somewhat secondary, for the grassroots efforts and active spiritual engagement conducted in weekly prayer and evangelistic meetings reveal the heart of a people who believe with full conviction that God is on the side of the undocumented.

What is lacking in the current scholarly conversations with regard to immigration reform are the experiences and voices of the undocumented Pentecostals and their Latino/a pastors, who have walked with them during these perilous times. Given the displacement of undocumented immigrants and the increasingly hostile climate propagated by heinous laws, such as the infamous Arizona SB 1070 and its Alabaman "demonic reincarnation" HB 56 (as some Latina/o Pentecostal pastors might view it), a thorough reflection from within the much-affected Pentecostal Latino/a church and

---

8. For a thorough discussion on the sources for developing an authentic Latina/o Pentecostal theology, see Villafañe, *Liberating Spirit*; Solivan, "Sources of Hispanic/Latino American Theology," 134–50; and Alfaro, *Divino Compañero*, 128–48.

community is to be expected. There is a great need to bring together the voices of Latino/a Pentecostal pastors to reflect on the reasons for the past passivity and lack of engagement with issues of immigration and political activism, and generate biblical and theological responses on immigration based on the lived experiences of the Latino/a Pentecostal community. Pastors and theologians need to embark on this project together in order to initiate a dialogue, which will spark action within Pentecostal churches to work for immigration reform in conjunction with Protestant and Catholic churches.

Questioning Pentecostalism's Political Conservatism

Seeking answers for the lack of political participation among Pentecostals in the struggle for immigration reform, I came across an open letter written by Daniel Ramírez to Arizona State Representative Steve Montenegro. The letter vividly captures the clerical sentiment and disdain for his turncoat political antics in view of his spiritual and cultural heritage. Throughout the letter, Ramírez makes use of biblical imagery from the immigrant stories in the book of Ruth and alludes to the death-threatening experience of the Jews in the time of Esther. Ramírez paints quite a picture:

> I write with great disappointment over your betrayal of people who counted on you to stand up for them and over your greater concern for a bright personal political future in Arizona. As you well know, the community of apostolic believers who made it possible for your parents and family to enjoy a full life in the United States has always included a significant number of brothers and sisters who, like your family, have also journeyed in search of a full life, often away from very desperate situations, obeying a "higher law" of survival. Unlike you, they did not have the privilege of official documents from a denomination (Apostolic Assembly) to ease that transition. All they had was a name written in the Lamb's Book of Life and, often, a letter certifying to good Christian character from an apostolic pastor in Mexico or Central America. Yet, as faithful payers of tithes and offerings and untold hours and years of religious labor, they made possible the sustenance of your ministerial family after its arrival from El Salvador.[9]

9. Ramírez, "Open Letter."

This letter finishes with a stern denunciation of Montenegro as he is antitypically compared to Esther, who was a heroine for her people in saving them from the evil plans of wicked Haman. Ramírez lucidly establishes the contemporary situation of Latinos/as in Arizona by overlaying their experience in parallel to the experience of the Jews in Esther's day. Through his cultural exegesis of Esther's story the types and antitypes become quite clear. Ramírez comments: "Now, like the beleaguered and criminalized community in the Book of Esther, your brothers and sisters must seek refuge from the blistering heat of xenophobic and scaremongering laws, appealing to high heaven for help in a time of trouble."[10] Noting the similarity between Haman's charges against the Jews (i.e., they are considered law-breaking immigrants), Ramírez points to Senator Russell Pierce as "Arizona's own Haman." Then, he prophetically rebukes Montenegro for not having the courage to be an Esther for his own people. Instead of siding with the undocumented, Montenegro has stood shoulder-to-shoulder with the Hamans of this day in order to advance his own political career. For Ramírez, this is doubly hypocritical, because as a church leader he undoubtedly transported so-called "illegal aliens" and surely received (and perhaps continues to receive) financial assistance in the form of tithes and offerings throughout his ministerial trajectory.

Reflecting upon this tragic tale of political thirst for power, which surprisingly turns a blind eye to justice and the great need for immigration reform, one has to consider the allegation that the Pentecostal church in general and Latino/a Pentecostals in particular have not characteristically participated in political action due to its traditional conservative affiliations and over-spiritualized practice of religion.[11] Historian Luis Rivera-Pagán describes it like this:

10. Ibid.

11. Perhaps the most famous and often quoted assessment of the lack of political awareness within Pentecostalism has been articulated by Christian Lalive d'Epinay in his *Haven to the Masses*. Gleaning from a socio-scientific perspective heavily influenced by deprivation theory, Lalive d'Epinay caricatured Chilean Pentecostalism as living out a "pie-in-in-the-sky" existence fueled by an over-spiritualized understanding of the Christian faith, which left devotees with little interest in social concern. In a similar manner, in *Vision of the Disinherited* Robert Mapes Anderson argued that early Pentecostals' millenarian understanding of the imminence of Christ's return led them to retreat from all worldly concerns. For Anderson, this ecstatic escape sought to ameliorate their condition as social outcasts, which in turn led to the social passivity of the movement. However, what these studies fail to grasp is that, though the masses turned to Pentecostalism seeking spiritual refuge, at the same time they were involved in various forms of faith-based

In the mid-twentieth century the community of the saints stressed separation and distinction from the world, functioning as a refuge from its sorrows and temptations. When prompted and challenged to confront controversial and political social matters, most evangelical and Pentecostal churches would quote Jesus' words to Pilate as the legitimizing text for their political abstention: "My kingdom is not of this world" (John 18:36).[12]

Yet, Rivera-Pagán is quick to point out this reading of supposed disinterest in politics by Pentecostals dismisses their involvement in other activities, which are viewed as less politically inclined. Unlike the Latino Catholic church, with its explicit social and politically engaged agenda,[13] it could be argued the Latino/a Pentecostal church has typically shied away from political involvement and social activism.[14] In part, the reason for this supposed negligence is grudgingly Pentecostalism's conservative political stance, which for the sake of family and biblically based values at times ignores other important social concerns affecting Latino communities.[15]

---

activism, which sought to bring about change in their neighborhoods and cities. For a more critical analysis of these views and a helpful exploration of the complex sociological and political ethos of Pentecostalism, see Wingeier-Rayo, *Where Are the Poor?* 20–34; and Cleary and Stewart-Gambino, eds., *Power, Politics, and Pentecostalism*.

12. Rivera-Pagán, "Pentecostal Transformation," 202.

13. Among other essays, a great example of this is Chavez's chapter entitled "Hispanic Ministry and Social Justice," 155–71.

14. It must be noted that by "political involvement and social activism" I am referring more to direct participation in activities where civil disobedience is employed as an instrument for political change. Although there are examples of individuals, local congregations, and church denominations that have sought to engage in acts of civil disobedience within a Latino Pentecostal context, this has not been the norm. As I will demonstrate below, Latino Pentecostalism has always been actively involved in faith-based social action through the ministry of the local congregation and individual involvement in service to the community through participation in homeless shelters, gang-related outreach, and assistance to immigrant families. This line of community organizing and service is well documented in the following three chapters of the same edited book: Ramírez, "Public Lives," 177–95; Ríos, "Ladies Are Warriors," 197–217; and Espinosa, "Latino Clergy," 279–306.

15. In a chapter of his edited book, Gastón Espinosa challenges the notion that Hispanic Pentecostals register and vote as Republicans like their Anglo counterparts. Espinosa demonstrates that although Hispanic Pentecostals maintain very conservative core values, which are more consistent with Republican ideals, they have identified and voted as Democrats in the past three Presidential elections at the time the book was published in 2008. For example, in 2000 the Latino Pentecostal/Charismatic vote is broken down by political affiliation as follows: 47% Democrat, 20% Republican, 30% Independent, and 3% other. These and other poignant statistics point to the political awareness and

But, has the Latino/a Pentecostal church been silent and irresponsive to the plight of the immigrant? On the contrary, it has continually been a beacon of spiritual hope for immigrants as they traveled north across the desert in search of life and a great resource for helping them to establish themselves in the U.S.

Pentecostal Theological Models for Advancing Immigration Reform

The early accounts of the birth of Pentecostalism in the U.S. at the turn of the twentieth century testify to the participation of Hispanic immigrant communities. From the outpourings in Topeka, Kansas to the Azusa Street Revival—from which various Pentecostal denominations later developed—there are significant evidences of the participation of Hispanic immigrants within the leadership and missionary activity connected to these movements.[16] Carmelo Álvarez documents the often-unmentioned presence of Hispanic converts and missionaries in the early period of the Pentecostal movement.[17] Taking this cue, Eldin Villafañe argues the presence and participation of Hispanic Pentecostals in the early days of the Pentecostal movement warrants a closer look at the "symbols of resistance, survival and hope," which can be investigated by examining the activities of its key leaders and preachers.[18] In addition, Villafañe uses the term "spirit of the oppressed" to refer to the subversive and liberating activities of various Pentecostal leaders and evangelists in order to demonstrate their commitment to immigrants in their service to the Hispanic community.

In a similar vein, Daniel Ramírez argues Pentecostals' advocacy on behalf of immigrants has not taken the typical approach as that of U.S. Latino

---

self-realization by Latino Pentecostals that the Republican Party aligns well with their spiritual values but does not present solutions for their pressing economic needs and cry for immigration reform. See Espinosa, "Latinos, Religion," 251.

16. Victor De Leon preserves the testimony of the silent Latina/o Pentecostals who were present at Azusa Street in the following quote (author's translation): "no one was surprised to see Mexicans in the meetings at Azusa Street, although there number was not great. Many of them were wealthy ranchers and very devoted Catholics. Notwithstanding, some had arrived recently from Mexico and by this time they found themselves as expatriates in an environment controlled by the American culture and language." *Silent Pentecostals*, 29.

17. Alvarez, "Hispanic Pentecostals."

18. Villafañe, *Liberating Spirit*, 90.

Catholic congregations, yet the reality is that Latino Pentecostal congregations have always helped documented and undocumented immigrants spiritually, economically, and hospitably. Moreover, whereas it is far easier to document the participation of Catholic and Protestant church involvement in the Sanctuary Movement during the '80s, the Latino Pentecostal church involvement was not as evident.[19] Although no official involvement at the denominational level could be established, according to Ramírez, "the refugee praxis of Latino Pentecostal churches manifestly proceeds from an intuitive response of the heart."[20] Thus, if we are attempting to establish an authentic theological response to the current immigration debates from a Latina/o Pentecostal perspective, their Spirit-led pro-immigration reform praxis should form the basis for their biblical and theological social ethic.

It must also be said that, because of the absence of Hispanic representation in the top leadership of the main Pentecostal denominations, historically there has been a lack of organization to officially call for immigration reform and present a unified denouncement of unjust immigration laws by interdenominational coalitions. Although the transnational fluidity of early Pentecostal Hispanic immigrant missionaries reveals the concern for the church to connect with its Latin American ecclesial counterpart even at the expense of losing or jeopardizing their legal residence in the U.S., only recently have Pentecostals come together within their own denominations as well as with others in efforts to advocate for immigration reform. Yet, instead of waiting for an official declaration by the head overseer or the executive committee of the Anglo denominations that most Hispanic Pentecostal congregations serve under, we would do well to identify within our own popular tradition and experience biblical and theological models for advancing immigration reform, which have been developed and shaped in the struggle to find a place and identity for our family and church.

Spirit-led Hospitality of Welcoming the Undocumented

Considering the reality of ecclesial and political under-empowerment in which the U.S. Latino Pentecostal church finds itself, it is no wonder that historically few Pentecostals actively engage in civic marches and protests

19. Espinosa et al., "Introduction," 11. In addition, Michael D. Matters' study of 371 declared sanctuary congregations up to the year 1988 establishes no official Pentecostal church involvement in the Sanctuary Movement (Matters, "Sanctuary Movement").

20. Ramírez, "Borderlands Praxis," 592.

in favor of immigration reform. Gastón Espinosa notes that "the primary institutional sponsors of faith-based community organizing are Catholic, moderate and liberal Protestants, and black Baptist and historically black congregations."[21] But it would be a mistake to equate the absence of Latino Pentecostals with a complete disdain for civic engagement. What the Latino Pentecostal community has lacked at a denominational and organizational level, they more than make up for it at a local grassroots level. There is no denying the Latino Pentecostal church has been an abundant resource for immigrants spiritually, economically, and socially.

The central thrust of the Pentecostal faith is the empowerment produced by the infilling of the Spirit with power as first evidenced in Acts 2, and more recently in the outpourings that gave birth to the modern Pentecostal movement. But contrary to the pie-in-the-sky outlook with which Pentecostals have customarily been categorized, the Pentecostal movement has always understood its Spirit-empowered evangelistic mission as including the social dimensions of the Gospel. The healings and deliverances read about in the book of Acts become the expected signs of the kingdom that at times initiate the convert into the Christian faith. Other times, in borderlands Pentecostalism these experiences provide opportunities for ministry among immigrant families who are struggling to secure food, shelter, and legal residence in the U.S. The Latino Pentecostal church must never forget the immigrant experience, which is vividly portrayed in their sermons, songs, and testimonies.

Harkening to his Pentecostal hermeneutical imagination, Daniel Ramírez contextualizes the ancient story of biblical Naomi in a way that depicts the struggle of the modern-day immigrant. Ramírez summarizes: "An economic refugee, whose subaltern status and plight as an older woman has worsened with recent widowhood, Naomi assumes a new identity upon return to her community of origin."[22] In short, Naomi is presented as a *bracera fracazada*: a migrant worker who has crossed the border and returns to her homeland having lost everything. But returning with her is an undocumented Moabite woman who ventures on beginning a new life together with her mother-in-law.[23] Ramírez's contextual reading of the text

21. Wood, "*Fe y Acción Social*," 152.

22. Ramírez, "Call Me 'Bitter,'" 40.

23. The undocumented status of Ruth can be established by recognizing she had no protection under the Mosaic Law to return to Israel. In fact Naomi insisted the two daughters-in-law return to their homeland and the house of their fathers: "Turn back, my daughters, why will you go with me? Do I still have sons in my womb that they

serves to highlight the typical Pentecostal manner in which this biblical passage is interpreted and preached. Naomi and Ruth's depiction as migrant workers who return defeated vividly connects with Pentecostal communities, who have immigrated to the U.S. seeking the American dream only to encounter the immigrant nightmare due to financial instability and marginalization. But just as with the biblical narrative of these women, Latina/o Pentecostals approach their everyday lives filled with faith in a God who provides for the sojourner.

Indeed, at the core of this Jewish immigrant tale stands the Old Testament social ethic of welcoming the stranger as established in Moses' law. God made provision for the incoming stranger, who was placed in a predicament of great need, and instructed the Hebrew people to take care of them on the basis of once having being strangers themselves. Leviticus 19:33–34 declares: "When a foreigner resides among you in your land, do not mistreat them. The foreigner residing among you must be treated as your native-born. Love them as yourself, for you were foreigners in Egypt. I am the LORD your God" (New International Version). It is remarkable to note that the Pentecostal community has not needed formal theological explanations to be convinced of the ethical command to care for the strangers in our midst. In fact, the Pentecostal intuition naturally responds to this biblical principle in their accompaniment of the immigrant within the congregation through visible and tangible acts of solidarity. The Naomi's and Ruth's who cross the southern borders of the U.S. illegally enter with a hope of finding an opportunity to work and provide for their own.

In modern times, Pentecostal congregations help documented and undocumented immigrants alike by becoming Spirit-led border communities who offer financial assistance, help with translation, assist them in finding jobs, and even provide work illegally. Gleaning from my own family's immigrant experience, I can testify to the care, provision, and guidance Pentecostal churches and pastors have offered immigrants throughout their journey to the north. Countless testimonies could serve to illustrate the solidarity of being a community, which sends, receives, and helps the immigrant. An example of the assistance Latino/a Pentecostals have given to immigrants in their struggle to survive is an episode that took place within my family in the early eighties.

---

may become your husbands?" (Ruth 1:11; New Revised Standard Version). Had Naomi thought Ruth and Orpah had a good chance to immigrate legally to Judah she would not have dissuaded them from following her. It was only after Boaz negotiated the purchase of the land of Ruth's ex-husband that she became a legal resident.

About mid-day during a hot summer month in Phoenix, a person knocked at the door of our family home. We later found out it was a Salvadoran refugee, who had traveled across Mexico and crossed the border illegally. He had been wandering the streets seeking food, shelter, and work. After many days of being unsuccessful in his quest, dehydrated, sunscorched, and losing hope, he came into our neighborhood and started knocking on doors. I remember my father was at work and my mother answered the door. After hearing his story and seeing his condition, she invited him into our house and offered him water and food. That afternoon when my father came home they talked and decided to give him shelter until he could find work. Why did they do it? How could they be so trusting to a complete stranger? The answer was simple: they were once aliens and the church had helped them out when they needed it the most.

Before immigrating to the U.S. in the '80s my parents, Quirino and Alicia Alfaro, and two older sisters had entered illegally in 1971. After struggling for weeks unable to find a job, in typical Pentecostal fashion my father went to church on a Sunday to ask the Lord for help and direction. Monday he had a job. The church connected him to a restaurant owner, who offered him a job as a dishwasher. This same tale of Spirit-led survival continues to be lived out by Pentecostals who immigrate to the U.S., and because of this experience Pentecostal communities live in genuine solidarity with undocumented immigrants. As I note elsewhere,

> Speaking from a southwest borderlands immigrant perspective, we were formed, and continued to be formed, by the struggles of the immigrant journey. While living here in a state of ambivalence, of being "*ni de aquí ni de allá*" (neither from here nor from there) and struggling to adapt to American culture, the experience of Latinos in general, and those living in the Southwest borderlands in particular, can best be described as "unempowered." From this "underempowered" position, various religious strategies have been put in place implicitly or explicitly in order to ameliorate the living conditions of our so-called "alien" status. For Latino/a Pentecostals, this strategy means walking in the presence of their Lord and Savior through the Spirit.[24]

Indeed, this same Spirit-led practice of welcoming the undocumented stranger is the typical hospitality Latina/o Pentecostal parishioners have offered and continue to offer countless immigrants on account of their faith.

24. Alfaro, *Divino Compañero*, 145.

Rev. Ángel Marcial, administrative bishop of the Church of God Southeastern Hispanic region, explains what this kind of hospitality entails:

> This is a hospitality that doesn't understand discrimination, pressures, deportations, or dispersions. It understands that all borders and barriers that separate us are broken through Christ.
>
> The "immigrant situation" becomes a calling for us to fraternize more, similar to the situation at Pentecost, where any differences were harmonized by the Spirit. When our charity is genuine, it leads us to true acceptance of one another. Through the Pentecostal experience, we can manifest understanding and comprehension of diversity in an ethical way.[25]

At every service, prayer gathering, or home Bible study, where Latina/o Pentecostals come together in spiritual solidarity, there will certainly be a time to pray for those in financial distress, those who need jobs, and the undocumented in their midst who are hoping for a change in immigration laws.

Such was the experience of my paternal grandfather, who entered the U.S. illegally for the first time some time in the '60s. With a family in great need and being the only breadwinner, he crossed the border only to soon come back home defeated and in despair. Following the prayerful advice of my grandmother, he determined to try his luck again in *El Norte* ("the North," i.e., the U.S.). After crossing the border, he found some money on the dirt road he traveled and became convinced God was on his side. For the next weeks he worked as a *bracero* and saved up some money until he became gravely ill. Considering the possible advice his praying wife would give him, he realized what he needed to do. He sought a Pentecostal church and, upon hearing the sermon, he rededicated his life to the Lord and received divine healing. From that day forward, the immigrant Pentecostal community who worshiped in Spanish gave him hope and peace as he lived far away from his loved ones and fostered in him a sense of divine providence, despite the uncertainty of his work and residential status.

This is what the Latina/o Pentecostal church continues to offer documented and undocumented immigrants alike today: a hope for a better future, which is grounded in the faith in a God who still provides for the sojourner. This Latina/o Pentecostal practice is grounded not only in the Old Testament social ethic of caring for the strangers (read as "illegal aliens" or, better, "undocumented")[26] among us, but also in the New Testament

---

25. Marcial, "Hispanos y la Inmigración," 18.

26. See Castelo, "Resident and Illegal Aliens," 65–77.

practice of hospitality, which in the Pentecostal ethos takes on particular spiritual significance. Indeed, Latina/o Pentecostals literally see themselves obeying the author of Hebrews' command to be hospitable on the biblical basis of unwittingly entertaining angels (Heb 13:2). Thus, in the Latina/o Pentecostal imagination not only do the Old Testament narratives serve as models for modern-day hospitality, the New Testament establishes it as the correct response toward the immigrants in our midst, regardless of official immigration status.[27]

Pentecostal Preachers as Prophets for Immigration Reform

Perhaps one of the main reasons for the Spirit-led hospitality of the Latina/o Pentecostal church is the connection between pulpit and practice within the congregation. Pastors and preachers within the Pentecostal tradition possess an authority and power of persuasion that leads the parishioners to step out in faith in service to the other. Indeed, the role of preaching in the Pentecostal community is a major contributor either to the apathy or to the increased participation of the congregation in social and civic political action. When a local preacher, pastor, or evangelist does not engage the congregation with challenging sermons seeking to awaken the church to socio-political participation, the flock will remain disinterested and lack the desire to actively participate in the pro-immigration efforts of the wider Latina/o community.

In this regard, the Latina/o Pentecostal church would benefit from the recovery of past preachers and recognition of some present ones, who have become true prophets for immigration reform. Toward this end it might serve as a good reminder to acknowledge the link between the great immigration activist César Chávez and the Pentecostal community, which early in his career influenced him positively. In his own words, Chávez retells his testimony of participating in a Pentecostal worship service like this:

> After they started their service, I asked if I could join them. In those days there was a lot of separation between Protestants and Catholics; in San José I was one of the few Catholics who attended Protestant services. When we first came to *Sal Si Puedes* [the San José barrio] Protestants were the ones who gave us lodging and food and invited my mother to the services. She wasn't afraid of

27. For an illuminating study on hospitality from a Pentecostal and interreligious perspective, see Yong, *Hospitality and the Other*.

> them. So in that little Madera church, I observed everything going
> on about me that could be useful in organizing. Although there
> were no more than twelve men and women, there was more spirit
> there than when I went to mass where there were two hundred.
> Everybody was happy. They were all singing. These people were
> really committed in their beliefs, and this made them sing and clap
> and participate. I liked that.[28]

Significantly, the reference to the Protestant church here points to a local Pentecostal congregation that met at the home of a pastor whom Chávez was helping with his immigration status.[29] Although the true spiritual influence that inspired Chávez to become the leading social prophet was his Chicano Catholic popular religiosity, his chance encounter with the worship of Protestant (Pentecostal) churches led him to incorporate *corridos* (popular Mexican ballads) in his union meetings and rallies.[30]

From Latino Pentecostal pulpits across the U.S. the message of the Gospel has been preached in a manner that resonates with the social implications of Jesus' inaugural sermon in Luke 4:18–19. Samuel Solivan summarizes it like this: "From a Pentecostal perspective, the preaching of the gospel is the most politically and socially radical activity the world has known."[31] Although at times the focus has been more on issues of social liberation, the Latino Pentecostal movement has a rich tradition of preachers who have actively participated in community organizing and various other activities aiming to mobilize the church in the Latina/o struggle for immigration reform.

A prime example of the emergence of the Pentecostal pulpit as engaging a prophetic civic activism is the work of Reies López Tijerina.[32] Although not addressing directly the social problems within the Latina/o community that point to the need for immigration reform, Tijerina's Pentecostal vision and active participation in politics as a Pentecostal preacher inspires a rethinking of the significant contribution Latina/o preachers could make by prophesying to crowds within and without the walls of the church. But, though much can be said of well-known Latina/o preachers

28. Garcia, *Gospel of César Chávez*, 135–36.

29. Ibid., 135.

30. Herrera-Sobek, "Farm Worker Hero," 25.

31. Solivan, *Spirit, Pathos and Liberation*, 145.

32. For a brief but penetrating study chronicling the life and work of Reies López Tijerina see Busto, "'Outer Boundaries,'" 65–75.

and evangelists who use their pulpits to inform and make poignant appeals for immigration reform and assist local parishioners with faithful hope, it is far more difficult to document the grassroots-level sermons of local pastors who oftentimes get little recognition.

For example, we could point to the preaching of Rev. René Molina, a Salvadoran-born pastor of a storefront church plant begun in the 1980s, which now consists of the 3,000 member-strong mega-church *Restauración* in Los Angeles. Molina's powerful appeal to Latina/o immigrants was recently documented in a newspaper article by *Los Angeles Times* correspondent Kurt Streeter: "'Jesus was an immigrant and outsider too,' Molina said, speaking in the Spanish of his native El Salvador. 'God is here in Los Angeles as you struggle. God is there with your family, in Mexico and Guatemala . . . Don't doubt your value, no matter what society says.'"[33] The article goes on to explain how Molina encourages his congregation to participate in politics by becoming citizens, voting, and taking part in pro-immigration marches. But the heart-felt Pentecostal appeal is not a mere biblically inspired sermon; it is a passionate call for participating in the American political system in recognition of his experience as an undocumented immigrant. Molina states: "I have crossed the border and felt the cold handcuffs. . . My journey permits me to have empathy, to understand."[34] All around the U.S., Latina/o Pentecostal pastors of small and large parishes almost unanimously unite with one voice to call their congregants to step up and act in favor of immigration reform by participating as voters.

A great example of how Pentecostal leaders and pastors preach on aspects of immigration within their churches is found in an article by Fidencio Burgueño, who at the time of writing was the Director of the Department of Hispanic Ministries within the Church of God. The article basically outlines a three-point sermon on a biblical response to the challenge of immigration for the church. Gleaning the Old Testament theme of the care Israelites needed to provide for the strangers in their midst, Burgueño makes the parallel appeal for the church today to respond to the challenge of immigration by understanding we will always have immigrants among us, and that we are commanded not to oppress them on the basis of once having been strangers ourselves.[35] Given the readership of this magazine (Hispanic Church of God pastors, leaders, and committed

33. Streeter, "Pentecostal Spirit."
34. Ibid.
35. Burgueño, "Los Inmigrantes," 4–5.

laity in local churches), one can certainly state that this homiletical outline is representative of the type of impact Pentecostal preachers and writers continue to make among congregations throughout the U.S.

Pentecostal Faith-based Civic Activism

Recognizing the influence of pastors and church leaders within the congregations, three leading Pentecostal denominations with a large Latino presence (Church of God, Assemblies of God, and the Apostolic Assembly of Faith) have recently sought to promote a wider participation of their constituents in pro-immigration reform via civic activism from a perspective of faith. In March of 2007, *El Evangelio* (the official periodical of the Iglesia de Dios, the Spanish-speaking arm of the Church of God with headquarters in Cleveland, TN) dedicated a whole volume to the issue of immigration, and more recently (Spring 2010) the topic headlined the bilingually published *Engage* journal, which is read by Church of God leaders across the world. Significantly, the latter issue contained an article titled "The Hispanic Blessing" by Raymond F. Culpepper, who at the time was General Overseer of the denomination.[36] Though most articles are largely focused on a missional understanding of the Latina/o harvest, they do present a shift in outlook in demonstrating where the church will need to be and how it will need to respond to the changing demographics in the U.S. In addition, the recent (2012) resolution concerning immigration released by the Church of God reveals the solidarity of the executive leadership with their Latino constituents.[37]

Within the Assemblies of God, there are also positive signs the denomination is doing more to participate in efforts for reforming immigration

---

36. Culpepper, "Hispanic Blessing," 18.

37. The text of the resolution reads: "the Church of God reaffirms its commitment to the following principles of a just process for immigration: 'that immigrants be treated with respect and mercy by churches; that governments develop structures that safeguard and monitor national borders with efficiency and respect for human dignity; that governments establish more functional legal mechanisms for the annual entry of a reasonable number of immigrant workers and families; that governments recognize the central importance of the family in society by reconsidering the number and categories of visas available for family reunification; that governments establish a sound, equitable process toward earned legal status for currently undocumented immigrants; that governments legislate fair labor and civil laws for all; and that immigration enforcement be conducted in ways that recognize the importance of due process of law.'" See more at: http://www.churchofgod.org/index.php/resolutions/resolution/immigration_2012.

laws in our nation. The official statement on immigration by the Assemblies of God reads: "As people of faith we support comprehensive immigration reform that reflects human dignity, compassion and justice integral to a 'nation under God.' Apart from issues related to governmental jurisdiction, we believe that the gospel of Jesus Christ compels us to minister to all who live or work within our country."[38] In addition, a recent article in the *Pentecostal Evangel* highlights the issue of immigration by pointing to the Pentecostal practice of welcoming immigrants. As a positive sign of what is to come, the article reports on initiatives the denomination is taking with regard to immigration in making coalitions with other denominations, churches, and faith-based organizations.[39] Such activity is indicative of the faith-in-action approach Pentecostal churches are turning to in more recent years.

Analyzing the present status of the churches, Ismael Martín del Campo, currently National Secretary of Christian Education of the Apostolic Assembly of the Faith in Christ Jesus (the oldest and largest Latino Oneness Pentecostal Denomination), provides a challenging rebuke for his church (and Trinitarian Pentecostals!) to heed the call to participate in immigration reform: "Expanding diaconal ministries and deepening the church's prophetic voice are also crucial next steps. The Apostolic Assembly is a church of immigrants, yet we hardly ever speak publically in favor of the thousands of undocumented immigrants that make up our congregations."[40] Following this quotation is a sharp critique for the church to denounce abortion clinics, and alcohol, tobacco, and casino industries, which in traditional Pentecostal fashion he perceives as representatives of the main social structures of sin in our nation. Significantly, though, at the top of this checklist of major immoral and corrupt social practices in the country is the issue of the unjust treatment of undocumented immigrants. It is this type of interior realization within the Latina/o Pentecostal church, which will ultimately lead it to understand itself as an important agent in societal change within the U.S.

If the above mentioned examples point to a hopeful changing trajectory within Latina/o Pentecostal church bodies, the next two examples provide concrete approaches to responding to the issue of immigration in a way that combines Pentecostal faith and political activism. There is no question today that the two leading voices pushing the Latina/o Pentecostal

38. The General Council of the Assemblies of God, "Statement on 'Immigration.'"

39. Kennedy, "Welcoming Immigrants."

40. del Campo, "Apostolic Assembly," 74.

church to become a more active participant in the political struggle for immigration reform are Rev. Samuel Rodríguez and Rev. Gabriel Salguero. Over the past couple of years these two evangelical pastors have been at the forefront of the dialogue between the leadership of our nation's political parties and the Latino evangelical church. Moreover, both have appeared in major national news networks promoting and advancing the need for immigration reform. Recognizing their rich Pentecostal heritage, Daniel Ramírez features their style of political engagement as a new wave of Latino Pentecostal faith-based civic activism.[41]

In October, 2010, Rev. Samuel Rodríguez landed on the front cover of *Charisma* (the leading Pentecostal/Charismatic magazine worldwide), heralded as "a voice for immigrants."[42] The featured article highlights the road taken by Rev. Rodríguez, an Assemblies of God pastor, to becoming a political advisor to President Barrack Obama and religious liaison with the Republican Party.[43] Under his leadership, the National Hispanic Christian Leadership Conference (NHCLC) has taken up a more politically active stand in favor of immigration reform. Before and after the election of President Obama, Rodríguez has been critical of the lack of action with regard to the promises Latinas/os were made concerning immigration reform.[44] This sharp critique of the failure of the present administration to solve the problem of immigration is an example of the political rhetoric and activity being advanced by the NHCLC. In his recent book, *The Lamb's Agenda*, Rodriguez remarks:

> The undocumented immigrant may present the most alienated and rejected segment of our society—today's "least of these." Although a divisive issue, Bible-believing Americans have a moral and biblical responsibility to bring Jesus to the undocumented. Evangelicals and Christians committed to spreading the gospel must incorporate prophetic witness that heals communities, ushers peace, and exalts righteousness and justice.[45]

This statement echoes Rodriguez's insistence that the church today should be defined by the effort to simultaneously preach spiritual righteousness

41. Ramírez, "Divino Compañero," 208–9.

42. Schweikert, "Voice for Immigrants."

43. Significantly, Rodríguez was among five religious leaders who were invited to provide invocations at the 2012 Republican National Convention.

44. Espinosa, "'Salvation and Transformation,'" 146.

45. Rodriguez, *Lamb's Agenda*, 100.

with the force of Billy Graham, and advance social justice with the determination of Martin Luther King Jr. in its quest to fulfill the Great Commission.

Perhaps more decidedly politically focused and ecumenically connected, Rev. Gabriel Salguero, a Nazarene pastor who grew up Pentecostal and is currently the president of the National Latino Evangelical Coalition (NaLEC), led the invocation at the 2012 Democratic National Convention. Recently, Salguero was a speaker at the 2014 Justice Conference in Portland, bringing a provocative and passionate talk to community organizers and social activists gathered from around the country. Salguero's key role as community organizer and speaker represents a new generation of Latina/o Pentecostal leaders who are approaching the fight for immigration reform by creating ecumenical networks focused on social and political activism.

For example, Salguero wrote an open letter to Arizona Governor Jan Brewer in which he poses biblical and theological arguments requesting her to veto SB 1070:

> The faith question: What does the Church or my faith have to do with it? Simply stated, as a Christian I am mandated to love my neighbor as myself without prejudice to origin, color, or creed. Jesus himself reminds Christians to "welcome the stranger" in Matthew 25. In addition, the Torah of the Hebrew scriptures reminds us continually to be kind and merciful to the stranger, widow, and orphan. In the end a nation is judged by how it treats the most vulnerable among them. My faith compels me to speak for and with the immigrants and their families. Love thy neighbor does not have a border limitation.[46]

His writing, speaking, and civic protests point to a new approach of Pentecostal faith-based civic activism, which embraces and promotes a desire for the greater Latina/o evangelical community to engage in acts of nonviolent civil disobedience in the struggle for immigration reform. Significantly, among the key leaders featured in the recent national campaign, *Fast for Families: a call for immigration reform and citizenship*, were Samuel Rodriguez and Gabriel Salguero. Thus, one may detect a spiritual impetus in both of these Latino evangelical leaders that is fueled by their deep Pentecostal faith and commitment to immigrants across America. For in the end, it is not a question of Pentecostal power or politics, but of learning how the two can be wedded together as we seek to act from a faith perspective that is anchored in our Pentecostal tradition.

46. Salguero, "Open Letter."

Conclusion

As a pastor and scholar, I have been impacted by the sense of displacement and insecurity recent immigration laws in Arizona have generated among the Latino community. Pastorally, this has led me to learn more about how to assist congregants who have been arrested and are waiting a court date for possible deportation. Along with a greater compassion for the undocumented and their families, these experiences have caused me to think deeply on issues of immigration from a biblical and theological perspective. We have lost families who have returned to Mexico or have moved to other states hoping for better financial opportunities. We have felt the pain of deportations, which have split up families in our congregation. Yet, we have also seen God's mighty hand intervene in cases where our parishioners were facing deportation but were miraculously released. We have also witnessed how God has worked through the current anti-immigration laws in Arizona to give residency status to a family in our congregation who felt led from God to turn themselves in to Immigration and Customs Enforcement.

As a pastor, I have come to realize that we can no longer opt out of political and social involvement within the greater Latino/a community. They need us as much as we need them. We need to form partnerships, pray, and come together with activists despite our political affiliations and even theological differences. As a growing Latino/a community of faith who serves a large segment of the undocumented population in the U.S., we need to be more politically informed and participate in civic demonstrations. This coupled with our spiritual and biblically based approach for sending, receiving, and helping the immigrant will enable the Latino/a Pentecostal community to be a more active agent in the struggle for immigration reform.

Discussion Questions

1. The author presents two questions as crucial to the discussion of church involvement in immigration issues. What are those two questions? Would you agree that these are the key foundational questions? If so, why? If not, why not?

2. According to this essay, what should be "the starting point for developing a theology of immigration grounded in the experience of the

Latino Pentecostal community," which often has been absent in scholarly discussions?

3. Is it fair to say that U.S. Latino Pentecostals have not stepped forward to help immigrants? How have Latino Pentecostals come to the aid of immigrants at the grassroots, local church level?

4. The author cites two biblical accounts that Daniel Ramírez contextualizes to the immigrant situation in Arizona. What are those two accounts? Did his biblical readings open up a new way of looking at those Old Testament books? If so, how?

5. What three Pentecostal denominations and which two national Hispanic organizations does the author cite to demonstrate the recent involvement of Pentecostals in the movement of immigration reform?

$$\text{------ 6 ------}$$

Towards an Hispanic Biblical Theology of Immigration

An Independent Evangelical Perspective

M. Daniel Carroll R.

Introduction

THE UNITED NATIONS INFORMS us that in 2013 there were over 230 million migrants or displaced people worldwide. This represents an increase of over 55 million since the year 2000. These numbers are staggering. The causes of this massive dislocation range from flight from wars, drug violence, catastrophic natural disasters and climate change, persecution (whether political, religious, or racial), and economic hardship to embarking on a trek to a new place simply to secure a better standard of living. Diaspora communities of immigrant groups are forming in developing countries as well as in more prosperous nations. This surging demographic is generating unexpected socioeconomic, political, healthcare, educational, and security challenges in the host countries, and the unforeseen changes in their cultural fabric are triggering anti-immigrant sentiments and legislation. A testament to the growing importance of migration are the multiple burgeoning fields of academic research into its many facets and the attempts around the world to formulate adequate local, national, regional, and international policies to cope with the changing landscape.[1] Although this volume focuses on immigration into the United States, particularly of

---

1. Note, e.g., Fiddian-Qasmiyeh et al., eds., *Oxford Handbook*.

Hispanics, the pressing, urgent realities are truly global. The scale and impact of contemporary migration are unprecedented.[2]

What kind of theological and missional sense can those of Christian faith make of these complex phenomena? The other essays in this volume approach the topic of immigration from the perspectives of diverse ecclesial and theological traditions, each of which has a particular way of understanding the character of God and Christian life (both individual and corporate) in the world. Each offers a different way of looking at migration and immigrants. Within Protestantism, however, there are thousands of churches, groups, and individuals that do not align themselves with any of these traditions or that adopt an additional descriptor within those traditions. I am referring to those who classify themselves as "evangelicals."

Evangelicalism must be described in a fairly general sense, as it is not confessionally or liturgically homogeneous[3] nor is it circumscribed by a single organizational structure.[4] Years ago British historian David Bebbington identified four shared commitments of the movement, a characterization that is now standard for research on evangelicalism.[5] These core elements are: *conversionism* (the need for each individual to place personal faith in Jesus Christ), *activism* (a commitment to proclamation and service), *biblicism* (the central place of the Bible for faith and practice), and *crucicentrism* (belief in the supernatural saving work of Jesus Christ on the cross). The ethnic diversity and global presence of evangelicalism is growing, and the weight of Majority World perspectives[6] and of minority views in Western evangelicalism grows apace.[7]

2. For global statistics, see http://www.un.org/en/development/desa/population/migration/publications/wallchart/docs/wallchart2013.pdf. For U.S. Hispanic immigration, see the periodic publications by the Pew Hispanic Center (www.pewhispanic.org).

3. See, e.g., Naselli and Hansen, eds., *Four Views*.

4. The National Association of Evangelicals (NAE) encompasses a wide swath of evangelicalism, but even it does not comprise all of the movement. The two largest associations of Hispanic evangelicals are the National Hispanic Christian Leadership Conference (NHCLC) and the National Latino Evangelical Coalition (NaLEC).

5. See Noll, "What is 'Evangelical'?" and McGrath, "Faith and Tradition," 19–32 and 81–95, respectively; cf. Bird, *Evangelical Theology*, and Larsen, "Defining and Locating Evangelicalism."

6. Jenkins, *Next Christendom*; idem, *New Faces of Christianity*. The Lausanne Covenant is the shared theological document to which evangelicals worldwide subscribe (http://www.lausanne.org/content/covenant/lausanne-covenant).

7. E.g., Rah, *Next Evangelicalism*.

This chapter is grounded in the second point of Bebbington's definition: the supremacy of the Bible to establish a position on any given issue. Our goal is to present foundations for an expressly evangelical *biblical* theology of immigration, instead of working within the parameters of a certain dogmatic or systematic theological framework.[8] In no way, of course, does this approach diminish the significant biblical work on immigration that is being done within other Christian traditions.[9] This chapter is not comprehensive; much more can be gleaned from the Bible than is offered here.[10] The following presentation is divided into three sections: the image of God, the mission of the people of God as it finds expression through law, and life as the people of God.[11] Each of these three sections provides a particular kind of theological lens for looking at immigration. Because of my training and work, the following exposition concentrates primarily on the Old Testament.

In addition, this chapter is committed to an Hispanic reading of the biblical text. In an important book, *Santa Biblia*, Justo González explains that five perspectives differentiate how Hispanics read the Scriptures: marginality, poverty, *mestizaje*, solidarity, and exile.[12] While all are important, the last is most pertinent to this essay. Hispanics in their sociocultural location in this country can feel like outsiders and hence can appreciate certain biblical texts in unique ways, precisely because of their status as "strangers in a strange land." Diaspora, in other words, is being appropriated increasingly as a lens for reading the Bible.[13] Hopefully, our brief survey of some

8. Within evangelicalism there has been an ongoing debate about the relationship between biblical and systematic theology. See, e.g., Carson, "Systematic Theology and Biblical Theology," 89–104; cf. McGrath, "Faith and Tradition."

9. E.g., from a Roman Catholic perspective, see Groody and Campese, eds., *A Promised Land*; Ruiz, *Reading from the Edges*; Cornell, *Jesus Was a Migrant*. Also note the Catholic contributions to Nguyen and Prior, eds., *God's People on the Move*.

10. For a more thorough study, see Carroll R., *Christians at the Border*. That book and this essay focus on the canonical biblical text. Technical critical works are beginning to appear, which try to reconstruct the hypothetical development of attitudes toward immigrants in ancient Israel, but that level of detail is beyond the purview of this essay and is not always conducive for articulating biblical theology. See, e.g., Achenbach et al., eds., *The Foreigner and the Law*; Awabdy, *Immigrants and Innovative Law*.

11. The Bible also has been used to argue counter to what is presented in this essay. Note, e.g., Hoffmeier, *Immigration Crisis*. Amanda Rose presents how different border groups use the Bible in *Showdown in the Sonoran Desert*.

12. González, *Santa Biblia*.

13. Note, e.g., Rodríguez, "Toward a Diaspora Hermeneutics," 169–89; Carroll R., "Reading the Bible," 3–26; Lozada Jr. and Segovia, eds., *Latino/a Biblical Hermeneutics*; cf. Ruiz, *Reading from the Edges*, and Cornell, *Jesus Was a Migrant*.

of the biblical material can demonstrate the depth and breadth of the Scriptures' relevance for the life of immigrants, specifically those from an Hispanic heritage.

The Image of God[14]

The place to start any biblical discussion on immigration is Genesis chapter one. That is, we must begin at the very beginning. In this opening chapter, the Bible reveals the incomparable power, wisdom, and graciousness of God in creation, the climax of which is the creation of humans in his image (1:26–30). All persons—male and female, and all ethnicities—are made in the divine image. This foundational truth should orient any Christian perspective on immigration. Media pundits often focus first and foremost on statistics or the legal status of foreigners to define them. Pejorative labels and characterizations, like "illegal alien" or "invading horde," can be the result. Genesis one moves us in a very dissimilar direction.

In the Genesis account creation occurs in six days. The thematic structure is illuminating. 1:2 informs the reader that, before God began his work, all was formless and void. In the first three days order is brought to the chaos by separating the light from darkness, the waters from the land, and the land from the sky (1:3–10). Then God fills the emptiness with vegetation, the stars, the sun and the moon, and all kinds of living creatures on the ground, and in the sky and seas (1:11–25). Six times, God evaluates his handiwork as "good" (1:3, 10, 12, 18, 21, 25). Everything is in its proper place, full of life, and functioning as it should under God's sovereign rule.

With the creation of humanity on the sixth day (1:26–30), all is now celebrated as "very good" (1:31). This is the seventh time (seven being the number of completion or perfection) the term "good" is used, and qualifying it with "very" adds more emphasis to the special significance of humans. They are unique and are the crown of God's work! But, in that ancient context, what would it have meant that humans are made in the divine image?

Two ideas are pertinent. On the one hand, in some cultures, the king was considered to be the image, or the representative, of the deity, and this connection would have been the source of his authority and power. Another way of conceiving images in the ancient world concerned royal foreign policy, as it were. Kings erected statues—that is, images—of themselves in distant territories as symbols of their rule and presence. Both of

14. For a more detailed discussion, see Carroll R., *Christians at the Border*, 45–51.

these perspectives inform the Old Testament narrative, but its thrust is profoundly different. First, being in the image of God is true for all humans, not just kings. The concept of special standing has been democratized. Second, to be made in the image of God means that humans are the representatives of the Great Cosmic King on the earth. But humans are not images of stone; they are living creatures!

In addition, while there are endeavors that humans share with the other creatures (to be fruitful and multiply, cf. 1:22), there are tasks that are given to them alone. Humans are to subdue and rule the earth (1:26, 28). In chapter two, this command is expanded to include working the garden and caring for it (2:15).[15] What is more, although the creation had been deemed "good," it was not finished, as the series of tasks given to humanity to tame, nurture, and develop God's creation makes clear. In other words, humans are to collaborate with God and continue his work. The stress is on the functional, more on what humans are *to do* than what humans *are*. They are to act as his vice-regents, fulfilling their mandate with God, for God, and under God.

Finally, humans are commanded to fill the earth (1:28; cf. 1:22). Said another way, geographic movement is part of what it is to be human. This does not mean that every human being must continually be on the go. Rather, it reveals that migration would characterize human existence and theologically is somehow connected with the divine plans for the world and humanity. The motivations to migrate and the numbers vary by context and era, but the impulse is embedded in our very fiber. Indeed, human history is the history of migration. This feature suggests that humanity accomplishes the charges to "subdue" and to "rule" the earth and its creatures and to "work" and "take care" of the garden as God's vice-regents as it moves across the face of the globe. In the divine economy, migrations are purposeful in relationship to God and the created order.

The theological themes of the opening two chapters of Genesis have multiple applications to the immigration discussion. I mention just a few. To start with, the creation of humanity in the image of God reveals the incomparable worth and the infinite potential of all human beings, even immigrants! This foundational truth bears communicating in diaspora

---

15. These two verbs of 2:15 also appear in liturgical contexts. The first in reference to the Levites serving God in the tabernacle (e.g., Num 3:7–8; 4:23–26); the second in reference to obeying religious duties (e.g., Lev 18:5) or guarding the tabernacle (Num 1:53; 3:7–8). This suggests a religious significance to human administration of God's creation, his cosmic temple.

situations, where migrants and their communities can be seen as inferior by the native born population; where they can be scapegoated as vulnerable, as unprotected outsiders, strangers in a new, foreign, and intimidating land. Immigration ultimately is about people, valuable in God's sight. This perspective should govern how Christians, individually and corporately, perceive the sojourners in their midst, minister to them, and communicate their worth to the broader society. At the same time, immigrants should recognize and embrace their inherent significance and live into their God-given capacities, not absorbing the surrounding environment's demeaning of their persons. This is a challenge for Hispanic immigrants, many of whom may be undocumented and feel forced to live quietly out of sight. Living in the shadows can create an overwhelming complex of inferiority that can play itself out in destructive ways within the home, school, or work.

The mandate to fill the earth, which launches humanity's persistent wanderings, should stimulate reflection on a theology of history that encompasses migration as a constituent element. Within God's involvement in human history and the context for the mission of his people migration always has had a place. What we are seeing today, even if its scope is overwhelming, somehow is relevant to divine purposes. Majority culture Christians and their churches should involve themselves in outreach to immigrants and in seeking constructive action on their behalf, believing that such participation reflects the sovereign will of God. At the same time, immigrants should ask themselves how their arrival might fit into God's plans. Increasingly, Hispanic churches are getting a vision of launching themselves into their communities and offering social services to their members and others. Many Hispanic pastors also see their churches as means to reenergize the broader Christian church and to re-evangelize the country that in the past sent missionaries south of the border and once was a beacon for the worldwide church.

In summary, this opening section provides fundamental building blocks for a biblical theology of immigration. Genesis, chapters one and two, reveal most basically that immigration is about *people*, created in the image of God with all of what that entails in terms of worth, potential, and responsibility. What is more, contemporary movements are another chapter in the ongoing history of migration. Although confusing and immensely complicated, migration today lies within the purview of the sovereignty of God. This truth should encourage Christians of both the host and immigrant communities, respectively, to appreciate the arrival of newcomers and the journey here as connected to what God is doing in the world today.

The Mission of the People of God and Immigration Legislation[16]

The key passage for defining the mission of the people of God in the Old Testament is Genesis 12:1–3. The literary structure of these verses communicates that, because the people of God receive his blessing, they are to be the channels of divine blessing to the rest of humanity.[17] Genesis makes clear that this blessing has both material (e.g., flocks, food, water, children, peace) and spiritual (relationship with Yahweh) dimensions.[18] If one connects this foundational concept of blessing to the giving of the Law later in the biblical narrative, it is evident that the Law, through the attitudes and demands expressed in its legislation, was to be a blessing to the surrounding nations. As Israel incarnated the divine ideals of an alternative society shaped by these laws, it would be a witness to the wisdom of Israel and its God (Deut 4:5–8).

Christopher Wright uses the term "paradigm" to explain the significance of this idea. By this he means that Israel's laws "constituted a concrete model, a practical, culturally specific, experimental exemplar of the beliefs and values they embodied."[19] That is, in its particularity the Law actually pointed to something beyond the nation of Israel and its restricted, temporal sociocultural context to more transcendent matters. Through the medium of the Law, the enduring moral demands of God would be lived out in tangible ways within that society. Ideally, it would have presented to the world of that era an example of what a social life pleasing to God might look like. This paradigm, in other words, was designed in part as a means of blessing the world. As the other nations construed their own legislation

16. For more details, see Carroll R., *Christians at the Border*, 79–100; idem, "Welcoming the Stranger," 441–61; idem, "Diaspora and Mission."

17. There is debate concerning whether the Hebrew verb (in the niphal stem) in 12:3 should be translated as a reflexive ("shall bless themselves": New Jerusalem Bible, New International Version note, English Standard Version note, Common English Bible note) or as a passive ("shall be blessed": New America Standard Bible, New Revised Standard Version, New International Version, English Standard Version). Our discussion opts for the latter.

18. See Carroll R., "Blessing the Nations," 17–34.

19. Wright, *Old Testament Ethics*, 68. See the full discussion on pp. 48–75, 182–211.

and sociopolitical structures commensurate to these values for their own setting, they would have experienced the grace of God in a special way. The same is true today, for our very different time and circumstances.

The component of the Law relevant to this essay is the attitude toward and treatment of the stranger it commanded. No other ancient law code has anything close to the number of laws or the moral framework vis-à-vis outsiders that the Old Testament Law does. Fundamental to this legislation concerning the sojourners in their midst was the recognition that, as a group, these outsiders were vulnerable.[20] To begin with, in the ancient world there were no government "safety nets" or formal social institutions to support the needy. Help in times of sickness, death, crop failure, childbirth, and the like had to come through the extended family. This, of course, is what immigrants lacked; they had left their extended families behind in their lands of origin. As a result, foreigners would have been dependent on the Israelites for charitable aid. Second, in a peasant economy like Israel's, land ownership was crucial for making a living and providing for one's family. According to Israel's laws, however, property was to stay within the family and passed down through the male heir (cf. 1 Kgs 21:1–3), thereby making it very difficult for outsiders to acquire land. Accordingly, they would have to look for work probably as day laborers on Israelite farms. Once again, the sojourner would have been dependent on Israelite kindness. In sum, immigrants were at risk. It is not surprising that the Law includes them along with the three other most needy groups of that society: widows, orphans, and the poor (e.g., Deut 10:18; 14:29; 24:17, 19–21).

The Law contains an impressive number of provisions to meet this vulnerability. In regards to labor, sojourners were to be allowed to rest on the Sabbath like everyone else (Exod 20:10; Deut 5:14), and they were supposed to be paid a fair and timely wage (Exod 23:12; Deut 24:14–15). Immigrants were not to be exploited in their work; they were not to be taken advantage of in their desperate efforts to survive. Legal proceedings were to be unbiased, and justice was to be the same for native born and foreigner alike (Deut 1:16–17; 24:17–18; 27:19). This would have been especially significant, as outsiders certainly would have been intimidated by the language and culture barriers of such settings. There also was a special dispensation

---

20. There are four Hebrew terms related to foreigners, not all of which are positive. The laws treated here were directed at the *gēr*, a label given to those who moved into Israel with the intention of becoming part of that community. English versions are inconsistent in their translations of *gēr*, using, for example, "alien," "sojourner," or "foreigner." Interestingly, the recent Common English Bible consistently renders *gēr* as "immigrant."

for immigrants to gather food at harvest time (Lev 19:9–10; Deut 14:28–29; 24:19–22). This is the stipulation that Ruth the Moabite took advantage of in her first days in Bethlehem (Ruth 2). Even more weighty, is that Israelites were to allow these foreigners to participate in community religious ceremonies, the most precious core of national life (e.g., Exod 12:45–49; Lev 16:29). Through this generous and benevolent legislation, the concept of the love of "neighbor" was being extended. The most natural understanding of this call in that culture would be to respond positively to a fellow Israelite in need (Lev 19:18), but this concern was broadened to include the foreigner. Israelites were to love the sojourner, not just their own kinsmen and countrymen, as themselves (Lev 19:33–34)! Outsiders would have been the most challenging neighbors to love, due to their being different.

There most likely were expectations for sojourners, too. At the most basic, they would have had to learn the language of Israel in order to work within and integrate themselves into their local communities. Some level of language acquisition would have been necessary, for instance, at the periodic public reading of the Law at which foreigners were to be present (Deut 31:8–13). These occasions would have afforded them the chance to learn the laws and cultural mores of their new land. Involvement in religious activities also probably meant that they would have converted to Yahweh, the God of Israel. In other words, the incorporation of immigrants into Israel carried expectations and required adjustments from all parties.

The question that would have arisen for Israelites would have been: Why be so open and welcoming to these newcomers? Two motivations are given. The first concerns historical memory. Israel had experienced oppression as foreign laborers in Egypt, whose religion and laws sanctioned that exploitation. In contrast, Israel's God and its Law would not countenance such mistreatment of the vulnerable. In the ceremonies celebrated in their homes and during the festivals at the sanctuaries, the people of Israel were to rehearse their past. They were never to forget what they had gone through (Exod 22:21; 23:9; Lev 19:18, 34; Deut 24:17–18). To do so could lead them to repeat that kind of injustice against those who had come in to dwell among them. This special historical memory was foundational to their self-understanding. Egypt was the site of their redemption under Moses; but it also was the crucible of their moral identity. They must not become the Egyptians.

The second, and most telling, motivation was grounded in the person and commitment of God himself (Deut 10:17–19). They were to "love" the foreigner, because Yahweh does, and he did so by giving them food and clothing. That is, God's love was concrete; it would meet the basic necessities of the sojourner. This assistance, though, was to come through the actions of the Israelites; they were to be the hands and channels of divine compassion. To aid immigrants, then, was to participate in the love of God for them. It presented a crucial choice to live as who they claimed to be, the people of God. Obedience to this mandate, in other words, was central to Israel's identity and responsibility; their attitudes and actions were truly to be a blessing to those who had come from elsewhere and would be a fulfillment of their mission.

This cursory look at Old Testament Law reveals that a biblical theology of immigration can inform legislation. Any value given to the immigrant must find tangible expression in law, and it is clear from the Old Testament that such legislation matters to God and should matter to his followers. Sooner or later, discussions on immigration have to get to the legal complexities of the entry, treatment, and integration of foreigners (and United States immigration legislation is quite a labyrinth of regulations!).[21] The Old Testament laws were quite broad and dealt with the daily challenges that these outsiders faced. This observation leads to a second point.

It is imperative to establish a values foundation for immigration legislation, and ultimately these find their source in God. The Old Testament starts with the basic human needs of these newcomers: work, legal protection, and food.[22] These laws were driven, not by strict controls concerning qualifications for entry and legal status or questions of national security (this was the impetus behind Egypt's laws; see in the next section), but by an appreciation of immigrant liabilities and limitations and the divine command to love the sojourner. This orientation, then and now, would generate laws characterized by compassion with an eye to the constructive incorporation of a new population into the community. It is not that organizing and protecting the border are bad or unnecessary. Rather, it is a question of what kinds of issues should be prioritized in the national debate and what ideals should inform the elaboration of every dimension of immigration

21. There are many resources online with this information. A helpful introduction directed at the Hispanic community is found in Cortés Jr., in collaboration with the Immigrant Legal Resource Center, *De inmigrante a ciudadano*.

22. These issues naturally move to the consideration of the relationship between legislation and fundamental human rights. While essential, that discussion is beyond the purview of this essay.

legislation, including border matters. Old Testament Law does not give us a blueprint for modern laws, but it can provide a moral compass.

In addition, the motivation of historical memory needs to be emphasized in the national debate. On the one hand, there remain mostly vestiges of the memories of immigrant groups that have made their way to the United States. Bits and pieces of these memories are visible in certain customs practiced at family celebrations (for instance, at birthdays, marriages, and Christmas) or in national holidays that find their roots in specific immigrant communities (e.g., St. Patrick's Day, the Irish; Oktoberfest, the Germans; Columbus Day, the Italians; Cinco de Mayo, the Mexicans). But these holidays are about parades, food, music, and drink. Forgotten are the marginalization, ghettoization, and exploitation of the first arrivals and their children. There is a national amnesia regarding the mistreatment in the past of each successive wave of foreigners to this country. This collective memory loss is combined with an idealized and sanitized history of immigration, whose symbols are the Statue of Liberty and the lyrical words by Emma Lazarus inscribed there. Consequently, negative reactions and nativistic laws have resurfaced today around Hispanic immigration. God's warning to never forget makes sense. To forget history is to repeat it.

This forgetting, however, also is evident within the immigrant community, especially among the undocumented. Seldom is the arduous journey to this country and the crossing of the border mentioned from the pulpit. Prayers may be offered for seeking employment or who are facing deportation hearings, but the migration experience itself is not mentioned within the confines of church sanctuaries. Perhaps this is done out of shame for lack of legal status or simply because immigrants would like to forget where they came from and how they arrived, because of this new start to their lives. In light of the biblical text, one must ask if something is not lost by trying to forget—that is, lessons about the guidance and care of God. Sadly, it is not uncommon for Hispanics, who have been here for a long time and qualified for amnesty under President Ronald Reagan in 1986, to be quite negative toward newcomers. They no longer recall their own original undocumented condition, nor do they consider that the benefits that they have accrued since then were gained through no actions of their own. Again, the wisdom of not forgetting the immigrant journey is manifest, even more tellingly, as legalized Hispanics discriminate against others from the same cultural background.

Third, and last, this cursory look at immigration law in the Old Testament demonstrates that the process of accommodating newcomers is bound up with mutual expectations. Israel was supposed to be gracious to the sojourner, but it was anticipated that the outsider also would make an effort to integrate into society. This process meant more than acquiring a job and lodging for oneself and one's family; it required getting involved in the community. Likewise, immigrants today should not come simply to see how they can take care of themselves and use the system to find employment. To move to another land and take advantage of its hospitality and its opportunities means also to invest in that society.

A biblical theology of immigration, therefore, must have an orientation toward immigrants as people made in the image of God and should provide moral (indeed, theological) guidance to legislation. This theology speaks to immigrant worth and responsibilities, with lessons for both the host and immigrant populations. A final component to consider is the contribution of Old Testament narratives to this biblical theology of immigration.

Diaspora Life under God

The Old Testament contains a number of accounts of movements of the people of God across boundaries.[23] These stories resonate with the experiences of many immigrants today. To read them is to quickly find striking parallels. Literary theory calls this dynamic interface between texts and readers the "merging of horizons" (the horizon of the world of the text with the horizon of the world of the readers). This engagement also can be explained as the projection of the mimesis of the Bible (that is, its presentation of the reality) "in front of the text" so as to intersect with and reshape the readers' perception of their world. On the one hand, this interplay between story and reality allows readers to feel at home in the text and claim it for their life. At the same time, the process challenges how readers understand their context. The Bible presents an alternative vision of reality, a picture of the "true" reality in God's sight that calls us to restructure our ways of seeing and acting in order to live into the vision. In this case, immigrant readers can learn through the Scripture to see their journeying as it "truly" is: a pilgrimage of faith under the sovereign eye and concern of God.[24]

23. For more details, see Carroll R., *Christians at the Border*, 51–74.

24. Note especially the various works of Walter Brueggemann. One of his seminal books was *The Prophetic Imagination*.

Much within the biblical narratives reflects perennial immigrant challenges. For instance, like today, the *motivations* to migrate in the world of the Bible could be the search for food (e.g., Gen 12:10; 26:1; 42:1–2; 43:1–2; Ruth 1:1), a fear of being killed (e.g., Jacob's fleeing from Esau to Padan Aram, Gen 27:41—29:14a; David from Saul, 1 Sam 20–27; Jesus and his family from Herod, Matt 2:13–18; the early Christians from persecution, Acts 8:1), or the desire to return to ancestral lands (e.g., Gen 31; Ruth 1:6–7; Ezra 1, 7; Neh 1–2; Dan 9:1–3). We also find examples of what scholarship now calls "forced exile"—that is, physical removal by another party to a different place. In the cases of Judah and Israel the most significant displacements occurred after the crushing invasions by the empires of the time (Israel by Assyria, 2 Kgs 17:6, 23; Judah by Babylon, 2 Kgs 25:11, 21, 26).

Several Old Testament accounts describe the *pressures* and *injustices* that mirror in some measure what immigrants currently experience. For instance, when Abram and Sarai and their extended family and servants travel to Egypt in search of food, they are willing to lie about their relationship to get across the border to find sustenance (Gen 12:10–20). Sarai is willing to put her bodily integrity at risk for the group, even as Abram can play the role of the protective brother to forestall potential compromises. Their ruse is a chancy ploy for survival; it is the sort of dangerous plan that immigrants around the globe contrive, when they find themselves in desperate situations.

A powerful account of unjust treatment and marginalization of foreigners is found in the opening chapters of Exodus. Frightened by the growing numbers of Israelites, which the Egyptians perceive as a threat to national security (Exod 1:9–10), draconian laws are put into place to control the male population (1:15–22). The following chapters portray the various common reactions to the complex drama of the presence of outsiders. There is the courage of the midwives and of Moses' mother to protect the children, the complaining and lack of faith of the Israelites who groan under unfair labor conditions, the compassionate embracing of the Moses child by Pharaoh's daughter and her servants, the ethnically and socially driven cruelty of the Egyptian taskmasters, and the irrational decisions of Pharaoh, the country's leader (a god, in the Egyptian national ideology). The illogical backlash against the presence of these descendants of the immigrant Jacob and his clan is evident as well in the decision to oppress the Israelites, while demanding they keep working to meet quotas under unreasonable conditions (finding their own straw to make the bricks). These sorts of negative reactions—whether personal, economic, or legal—illustrate the nativism that characterizes the reception of immigrants in a host country. The spectrum of treatment of the foreigner in Exodus, from the sensitive to the sadistic, has its counterparts in the tale of immigration into the United States and elsewhere.

Once in a new land, outsiders face the challenges of *integration* and *adaptation* to the different surroundings and culture. This difficult process of adjustment requires the ongoing, perhaps painful negotiation of possible losses: the loss of language, customs, foods, ways of dressing and acting, core values, even religion. Immigrants and their descendants have to decide what to retain from their land of origin and then develop strategies to preserve and pass that legacy on to the next generations. As they begin to accommodate themselves into their new setting, they may never know how their presence will influence in positive and constructive ways the host country. The dance of adjustment is difficult, but ideally both parties will benefit from the cultural engagement.

The Old Testament portrays various levels of accommodation of several individuals to their foreign surroundings. Joseph is a case in point. Once he is released from prison and established in Pharaoh's court, he is given an Egyptian name and an Egyptian wife (Gen 41:45). He would have to have been able to speak the Egyptian language to function as Potiphar's foreman and then later as a government official. Yet, surprisingly (or is it?) he gives his two sons the Israelite names Manasseh and Ephraim (41:50–52); he remembers his mother tongue (42:23), and asks for his bones to be taken back to the land of his birth when he dies (50:24–25). It also is impressive that he introduces his Bedouin brothers and father Jacob to Pharaoh, even though the Egyptians despised shepherds (43:32). In other words, although Joseph was a highly ranked, prominent person in Egypt, he was not ashamed of his cultural roots or his family. And then, the aged patriarch Jacob blessed Pharaoh (47:1–12)!

Ruth is another interesting example. Because of famine, Elimelech, his wife Naomi, and their two sons migrate from Bethlehem in Judah to Moab on the other side of the Dead Sea. Both sons marry Moabite women, one of whom is Ruth. In other words, Ruth marries an immigrant. After a number of years, however, Elimelech and the sons die (1:3–5). Naomi resolves to return to Bethlehem and tries to convince her daughters-in-law to remain in Moab and start a new life for themselves. Ruth chooses to go with

Naomi, but Orpah does not (1:6–18). Ruth, the widow of an immigrant, now becomes an immigrant to Judah.

The rest of the account of Ruth is the story of how she strives to find acceptance in Bethlehem. The start of her time there is awkward. Naomi is a bitter woman. She had lost the men of her family in Moab, and now she has come back with a Moabite daughter-in-law! When the two reach Bethlehem, Naomi does not introduce Ruth to the women of the town (1:19–21). Perhaps that Moabite immigrant stood awkwardly to the side, as the women embraced Naomi. Saying nothing and understanding little, maybe dressed differently than everyone else, surely Ruth felt out of place. Soon she goes to the fields to glean grain for herself and Naomi. After working all day no one knows her name or perhaps had even spoken to her; she is simply the Moabite who had arrived with Naomi. What the other harvesters do know is that she is a hard worker (2:6–7). This is the fate of so many recent arrivals: they are nameless and faceless, even as they are appreciated for their work ethic. Over time, Ruth gains the respect of Boaz, Naomi's kinsman, and becomes his wife (2:11–12; 3:10–13; 4:10). The elders compare her to the great women of Israel' past (4:11–12), and the townswomen, who earlier had ignored her, laud her love and loyalty to her mother-in-law (4:14–15). Her persistent efforts to carve out a place in Bethlehem have born fruit.

When Naomi hears the words of the women, she does not respond. Yet, she does take into her arms Ruth's young son, Obed, the one who would grow up to take care of Naomi in her old age (4:15–17). This little boy, offspring of a bicultural marriage between an immigrant and a native-born, never would have to struggle as his mother had in order to gain acceptance in that culture. Interestingly, the people of Bethlehem never call Ruth by her name. She is referred to as the "young Moabite woman" (2:6), "the woman" (4:11), "this young woman" (4:12), and "your daughter-in-law" (4:15). Even Boaz in public speaks of her as "Ruth the Moabite" (4:5, 10). In other words, she is part of the community, but not fully one of them. Not so Obed. Certainly, over time the community in accepting Ruth, the marriage, and the child (perhaps the first of several), slowly would have changed its view of outsiders.

The book of Ruth has a surprising ending. It closes with a genealogy that connects Obed to the lineage of David (4:17b–22). This immigrant peasant woman never could have dreamed that her move to Bethlehem would impact her adopted land like this. The New Testament extends the connection to the genealogy of Jesus, the Son of David and Messiah (Matt 1:5)! As more evidence of the impact of this immigrant woman's life, every year Jews read the book of Ruth during the Feast of Weeks (Shavuot). Immigrants can never know where they might fit in the plans of God for their families and for their new land. God may have surprisingly great things in store!

The very different attitudes of Ezra, Nehemiah, and Esther in exile testify to dissimilar levels of integration. Ezra, the priest, leads a return to the land for the purpose of reestablishing Israel as a law-obeying community. Assimilation into the Persian Empire is not a goal, although the Jewish homeland comprised the Persian province of Yehud. Ezra receives approval and material support from the Persian king Artaxerxes (Ezra 7:11–28), but his focus was on the unique identity of his people, not on intermingling with other ethnic groups. Nehemiah, on the other hand, as cupbearer to Artaxerxes, went to Yehud just for a time to complete the project of rebuilding Jerusalem's walls. He goes with imperial approval and aid, but in the end returns to the Persian capital to serve his king. For her part, Esther has no designs to return to Yehud. Through the contest to replace Queen Vashti, she becomes queen of Persia, and the plot of the book reflects Esther's growing conviction of the timeliness of her ascent to the position of queen to defend her people from deadly opposition in the empire. This descendant of immigrants becomes an instrument for good—and protection—in her adopted land.

Significantly, a sense of rootlessness characterized the life of the father of the faith, Abram/Abraham. Originally from Ur in southeast Mesopotamia, he traveled with his extended family to the northwest to Haran, before heading southward to Canaan (Gen 11:31—12:9). The only property he ever owned in that land was a plot of ground that he acquired to bury his wife Sarah (Gen 23). In one of Israel's ancient confessions (Deut 26:5) this nomadic clan leader is called a "wandering Aramean."

It is not surprising that the New Testament employs migration as a metaphor for the life of the Christian. In 1 Peter 2:11 the people of God are said to be "foreigners and exiles" (New International Version) in the world.[25] These are apt descriptors, because immigrants know what it means to be different, to live according to another set of criteria than that of their context, and to have dissimilar loyalties and another citizenship (cf. Phil 3:20; Heb 13:14). Immigrants understand this metaphor in their very being. For the native born, the metaphor may be an abstract concept, but for the foreigner, it is lived experience. In a sense, it might be said that the

25. For more details, see Carroll R., *Christians at the Border*, 103–21.

Christian church of the host country may need immigrants in their midst to be reminded of what it means to be strange, of what being a follower of Jesus entails. Sadly, many majority culture Christians have lost the sense of strangeness inherent in their identity and called for by the Gospel message; they rather like their surroundings and want to keep the strangers out!

What this selected survey of biblical material demonstrates is the relevance of its accounts for immigrants and for anyone interested in God's concern for them. The Old Testament, and to a lesser degree the New Testament,[26] provide vignettes of the *motivations, pressures,* and *processes of integration* of those who move to (or are taken to) new lands. In its pages immigrants read their own stories as if in a mirror, see how those ancient people on the move behaved, for good or for ill, and how they endured with God's help. These accounts offer, therefore, lessons of identity and faith. In sum, the Bible offers *a narrative theology of immigration,* a rich resource for migrant peoples. *¡Allí estamos nosotros en el texto bíblico! Nuestro Dios nos acompaña en nuestro peregrinaje* ("There we are in the biblical text! Our God walks with us in our pilgrimage."). The importance of religion is clear in the testimonies of many Hispanics, who have crossed the border. These, however, often are rooted in Latin American popular religiosity.[27] How much more powerful could be the stories of Scripture!

The Bible, of course, is not the only source of narratives that can encourage the immigrant to better understand their plight and potential. New films and documentaries provide opportunities for reflection and catharsis, even as they can educate the host culture of the difficult journeys and lives of outsiders. The realistic fiction of novelists, who have roots in both North America and south of the border or in the Caribbean, such as Francisco Goldman (Guatemala), Sandra Cisneros and Victor Villaseñor (Mexico), Edmundo Paz Soldán (Bolivia), Julia Álvarez (Dominican Republic), and Cristina Henríquez (Panama) portray the conflicted existence of immigrants and their descendants, who wrestle with how to handle their Latin American heritage and adapt to the United States. The cinema and the printed page forcefully and movingly depict the in-between life of the foreigner, who is neither home nor at home.

---

26. The strategy of the early church often entailed diaspora Christians beginning their work by speaking to diaspora Jews in their synagogues. See Ott, "Diaspora and Relocation," 73–94.

27. See, e.g., Hagan, *Migration Miracle*; Ferguson et al., *Crossing with the Virgin*; Daniel, *Neighbor*, 3–12; Chestnut, *Devoted to Death*.

Conclusion

This essay has argued for three important pieces that can serve to elaborate a fuller biblical theology of immigration. The first is the basic nonnegotiable truth that immigrants are made in the image of God. Hence, they have the same supreme worth and incredible potential as all other people, and likewise certain responsibilities before God. The opening chapters in Genesis also teach that migration needs to be woven into a theology of history.

The second component dealt with legislation. A biblical theology of immigration should impact ongoing discussions about immigration law, nationally and internationally. The Old Testament offers the moral framework for the content and purpose of this legislation: responding compassionately and concretely to immigrant vulnerability. Such an orientation, quite importantly, grows out of the heart of God. The third part of this initial foray into a biblical theology of immigration is narrative focused. The biblical accounts can encourage, sustain, and guide immigrants in their journeys to and processes of accommodation in their new land. At the same time, the biblical stories can serve majority culture readers as windows into immigrant realities.

There is much more that can be incorporated into a biblical theology of immigration. Hopefully, this chapter might encourage others in that effort, for the sake of the sojourner and in service to God.

Discussion Questions

1. What should be the foundational theological conviction in a biblical theology of immigration? What can it teach both the host culture and the immigrant?

2. What do you know about current immigration laws? What might be their underlying value and goal, as best you can understand?

3. How might Old Testament legislation regarding the sojourner differ— both in content and purpose—from what you know of current laws or those that are being debated?

4. Do any of the Old Testament accounts remind you of the experiences of family or friends (or even your own)? Which ones, and how?

5. Does your family have anything of immigrant memories in its food, celebrations, or stories? What parts of your family's immigrant past are you ignorant of? Why have they been forgotten? How might they inform how you engage the immigration discussion?

Appendix

A Comparative Table of Christian Traditions

Category	Roman Catholic	Lutheran	Reformed	Methodist/ Wesleyan	Pentecostal	Independent Evangelical
1) Historic or contemporary figure(s)	Pontificates of Pius XII (1939–1958), Paul VI (1963–1978), John Paul II (1978–2005), Benedict XVI (2005–2013), and Francis (2013–)	Martin Luther (1483–1546), Philip Melanchthon (1497–1560)	John Calvin (1509–1564)	John Wesley (1703–1791)	William J. Seymour (1870–1922) Eldin Villafañe, Samuel Soliván Reies López Tijerina, René Molina, Fidencio Burgueño Samuel Rodríguez, Gabriel Salguero	No key figure, but rather core elements of the movement: conversionism, activism, biblicism, and crucicentrism

Category	Roman Catholic	Lutheran	Reformed	Methodist/Wesleyan	Pentecostal	Independent Evangelical
2) Major theological themes	Holy Family as archetype of refugee family	Justification by faith as cause of good works	Establishment of just social order as part of Christian life	Methodological shift from ethics of legal obligation to ethics of character	Spirit-empowered evangelism with a social conscience (Book of Acts)	Image of God as foundation of biblical ethics
	Principle of solidarity	Two kingdoms or governments	Calvin as a refugee, exile, and resident alien	Restoration of image of God as goal of salvation and holiness	The world as the sphere of demonic action and divine intervention	Mission of God's people as expressed through the law of Israel
	Preferential option for the poor	Christians as "masks of God" in their vocations	Persecution and dispersion as mark of the church	Free will in each person to reflect God's moral image and strive for the state of perfection in Genesis	Separation and distinction from the world	Exile life and diaspora identity as God's people
	Migration as a sign of the church's universality and hope, and the unity of the human family	Christian as "world-person" and "Christ-person" (ethics of advocacy) and "Christ-person" (pacifist ethics)	Christian life as sojourn and exile		Spirit-led cries for justice in the world	Integration and adaptation of strangers to a strange land
			Diaconate church office for poor relief		Spirit-led grassroots hospitality	

Category	Roman Catholic	Lutheran	Reformed	Methodist/ Wesleyan	Pentecostal	Independent Evangelical
3) Biblical narratives	The Holy Family's flight into Egypt (Matt 2:13–23) Christ's identification with the strangers (Matt 25:31–46)	Looking for *posada* or inn (Luke 2:1–7) Sermon on the Mount (cf. Matt 5:39) Christian life in two realms, twofold citizenship (e.g., Phil 3:20, Eph 2:19; 1 Pet 2:14, Rom 13:1–7)	Concern for the poor and powerless (e.g., Matt 25:34–40, Ps 82:3) Repeated references to exile and asylum themes in Psalms (e.g., Ps 37:7–11) Office of *diakonia* in Book of Acts (cf. Rom 12:8)	Created in God's image (Gen 1:26–30) Christ teaches us to pray for our enemies (Matt 5:43–48) Christ in the vulnerable neighbor (Matt 25:31–46) Christ shows mercy while enduring evil (cf. Matt 27:15–25, Luke 23:34)	The story of Esther against Haman (Book of Esther) Naomi and Ruth as vulnerable *braceras* Jesus' healings and ministry of deliverance The power of the Spirit for a community-conscious evangelism (Acts 2)	Created in God's image (Gen 1:26–30) God's law as a blessing to the nations and the vulnerable (Gen 12:1–3; Deut 4:5–8) Diaspora life under God (e.g., Joseph in Gen, Book of Ruth)

Category	Roman Catholic	Lutheran	Reformed	Methodist/ Wesleyan	Pentecostal	Independent Evangelical
4) Selected sources	*Exsul Familia Nazarethana* (1952) *De Pastorali Migratorum Cura* (1969) *Erga migrantes caritas Christi* (2004) World Migration Day messages	*Treatise on Good Works* (1520) *Christmas Day sermon from Church Postils* (1521) *Temporal Authority* (1523) *Small & Large Catechisms* (1529) *Augsburg Confession* (1530)	*Ecclesiastical Ordinances* (1541) *Commentary on the Psalms* (1557) *Institutes of the Christian Religion* (final edition 1559)	Wesley's recollections of Aldersgate Sermons (e.g., *The New Birth*) Journal notes	Preaching and teaching of pastors Personal testimonies of divine intervention (e.g., to solve status of undocumented people) *Corridos* High-profile Pentecostal magazine and periodical issues on immigration	OT as moral compass and foundation for values for dealing with strangers NT use of migration as a metaphor for Christian life

Category	Roman Catholic	Lutheran	Reformed	Methodist/ Wesleyan	Pentecostal	Independent Evangelical
5) Historic or Contemporary Event(s)	Vatican II Council (1962–1965) Paul VI creates the Pontifical Council for the Pastoral Care of Migrants and Itinerant People (1970) U.S. Conference of Catholic Bishops' "Strangers No Longer" (2003)	Posting of 95 Theses (31 October 1517) Lutheran Immigration and Refugee Service (LIRS) traces its origins to 1939 Evangelical Lutheran Church in America's "A Message on . . . Immigration" (16 November 1998) Lutheran Church—Missouri Synod's *Immigrants Among Us* (November 2012)	Calvin's Reform in Geneva starts (1541–1549) Calvin meets Martin Bucer in Strasbourg (1538–1541) Perrin revolt (1555) John Knox's stay in Geneva (1555–1558) Establishment of General Hospital (1535) and French Fund (c. 1545) Presbyterian Church (USA) advocates for comprehensive immigration reform (2012)	Wesley's Aldersgate experience (24 May 1738) Wesley as member of Oxford's Holy Club (1729–1737) Wesley embraced the abolitionist position, wrote *Thoughts on Slavery* (1774) United Methodist Church's "Welcoming the Migrant to the US" (2008)	Azusa Street revival (1906–c. 1915) D. Ramírez's open letter to Arizona State Representative S. Montenegro (23 April 2010) Influence of Pentecostalism in Evangelical political activism (e.g., NHCLC, NaLEC)	Merging and parallels of biblical stories of migration with present-day immigrant readers' experiences Evangelical Immigration Table's "Evangelical Statements of Principles for Immigration Reform" (launched in June 2012)

Glossary

Aldersgate experience: Key turning point in John Wesley's life, in which he experienced the depth of God's salvation in Christ and committed to praying for his persecutors. The event took place during a meeting in May 1738 in Aldersgate Street, London.

Azusa Street Revival: Influential revival meetings in the early history of the Pentecostal movement that took place in Los Angeles, California (April 9, 1906—c. 1915), under the leadership of African American preacher William J. Seymour.

Borderlands: A physical or social space along one side or both sides of a border. The concept is often used to describe the dynamics of life in marginal regions or among marginalized groups vis-à-vis dominant centers of power (see *Mestizaje*).

Bracera/o: A Mexican worker admitted for a limited time to the U.S. for seasonal labor, especially in the agricultural sector. A controversial program due to its lack of fair wages and labor conditions for workers, the U.S. bracero program began in 1942 and officially came to an end in 1964.

Civil law: In theological usage, a term inclusive of all the laws of society, including those dealing with immigration. Because civil law offers a measure of order in society, it can be seen as God's gift. However, since such law is also formulated through the use of human reason, it can be fallible and must not be obeyed if it is contrary to God's will (see God's Law).

Corrido: A Mexican folk song that often describes heroic and legendary tales, or offers commentary on social issues such as drug trafficking, immigration, or life along the U.S.-Mexico border.

Diaconate: A church office of deacons or deaconesses, who are typically tasked with the care of the poor and other vulnerable neighbors.

Diaspora: A group of persons who live outside of the region or country where they or their ancestors previously resided. Reasons for diaspora or dispersion to other lands include fleeing from wars, drug violence, natural disasters, political or religious persecution, and economic hardship (see Reaspora).

Emigration: Leaving a region or country of which one is typically a native in order to live or settle somewhere else (see Immigration).

Ethics of advocacy: For Martin Luther, the way Christians make room for the law in the temporal kingdom, advocating for justice before the government to protect neighbors by restraining evildoers who have wronged them (see Pacifist ethics, Two Kingdoms).

French Fund: Established by wealthy French refugees around 1545, this Fund provided comprehensive poor relief for French immigrants and others passing through Geneva. John Calvin quietly contributed to this Fund for years (see General Hospital).

General Hospital: Established by laypersons in 1535, this social welfare agency focused its efforts on the care of poor Genevans by housing orphans, distributing food, and offering temporary shelter to travelers and refugees (see French Fund).

God's Law: God's will written in the human heart (natural law) and revealed to Israel in the Decalogue or Ten Commandments. It serves as a moral framework or compass for ethical issues (see Civil law).

HB 56: The Beason-Hammon Taxpayer and Citizen Protection Act is an anti-illegal immigration bill signed into law in the State of Alabama in June 2011. The U.S. Court of Appeals for the 11th Circuit invalidated some of the bill's provisions in August 2012 (see SB 1070).

Hispanic (Latino/a) Theology: A diverse body of theological reflections and writings from U.S. theologians, who claim recent or ancestral roots in Latin America, that engages themes such as marginality, poverty, *mestizaje*, solidarity, and exile (see Borderlands, *Mestizaje*).

Immigrant: One of various possible translations of the Hebrew word *ger*, which also is rendered in English Bible versions as alien, foreigner, sojourner, or stranger.

Immigration: Coming to a region or country of which one is not a native to settle there (see Emigration).

Liberation Theology: A theological approach with roots primarily in Latin American Roman Catholicism that sees liberation from systemic or institutional oppression (e.g., racial, socio-economic, political) and the practice of a preferential option for the poor as signs in the present that anticipate God's future salvation or coming kingdom. Diverse strands within Liberation Theology offered different structural alternatives for their contexts, and some within this broad movement opted to support revolutionary violence (see Preferential option).

Magisterium: The teaching authority of the Roman Catholic Church, especially as it is exercised through the Pope and the bishops.

Mestizaje: Historic racial mixing of Spanish and indigenous peoples, arising originally through the violent Conquest and Colonization of the Americas. The term is also used to describe the blending or hybrid character of racial and cultural identities, particularly in Mexican-American studies (see Borderlands).

Pacifist Ethics: For Martin Luther, the way Christians deal with each other and their enemies non-violently or with mercy and love in the spiritual kingdom, and therefore without seeking punitive justice or revenge from the government against enemies (see Ethics of advocacy, Two Kingdoms). Pacifism also is strong in Anabaptist circles and beyond.

Pontifical Council for the Pastoral Care of Migrants and Itinerant People: Established by Pope Paul VI on 19 March 1970, the Council is charged with the study and pastoral care of "people on the move," such as migrants, exiles, refugees, displaced persons, travelers, pilgrims, tourists, and students abroad.

Posadas: In some Hispanic Christian communities, a liturgical reenactment of the Holy Family's search for an inn (*posada*) for Mary and the baby Jesus to rest. The celebration serves as a preparation for Christmas and reminds Christians of the importance of faith in Jesus and hospitality towards strangers.

Preferential option: Extending the priority of Christian love to the poor and other vulnerable neighbors (see Liberation Theology).

Reaspora: Members of the diaspora who return to their—or their ancestors'—countries of origin (see Diaspora).

Sanctuary Movement: A campaign of civil disobedience against U.S. federal immigration policies on asylum during the early 1980s that led congregations across the U.S. to provide safe-haven for Central American nationals fleeing political persecution. Recently, a new sanctuary movement has begun to offer churches as refuge for immigrants who are in deportation proceedings.

SB 1070: Known also as Arizona State Bill 1070, the Support Our Law Enforcement and Safe Neighborhoods Act is an anti-illegal immigration measure signed into law in April 2010. In *Arizona v. United States*, the U.S. Supreme Court struck down three of its provisions as violations of the U.S. Supremacy Clause (see HB 56).

Second Vatican Council: Also known as Vatican II, this is the most recent Council of the Roman Catholic Church. It paid particular attention to that Church's relationship to the modern world. It opened in October 1962 under the pontificate of Pope John XXIII and closed under Pope Paul VI in 1965.

Two Kingdoms: Realms of God's ruling in the world whereby God justifies humans by forgiving their sins (spiritual kingdom) and promotes justice and peace among humans (temporal kingdom). Also known as the two governments in Lutheran theology.

Villancico: Spanish or Latin American Christmas carol with roots in the medieval era.

Vocation: In Lutheran theology, this is God's calling to each Christian to serve as instruments of divine blessing through their labors in family and marriage, economy and education, government, and church.

Bibliography

Achenbach, R., et al., eds. *The Foreigner and the Law: Perspectives from the Hebrew Bible and the Ancient Near East.* BZABR 16. Wiesbaden: Harrassowitz, 2011.

Adams, Mark, et al. *Bishops on the Border: Pastoral Responses to Immigration.* New York: Morehouse, 2013.

Adorno, Wilfredo Estrada. "A Wesleyan Pentecostal Theological Reflection to the Issue of Latino Undocumented Immigration." Paper presented at the Renewal in the Americas Conference, Regent University, Virginia Beach, VA, February 28–March 1, 2014.

Alfaro, Sammy. *Divino Compañero: Toward a Hispanic Pentecostal Theology.* Eugene, OR: Pickwick, 2010.

Althaus, Paul. *The Ethics of Martin Luther.* Translated by Robert C. Schultz. Minneapolis: Fortress, 1972.

Alvarez, Carmelo. "Hispanic Pentecostals: Azusa Street and Beyond." *Cyberjournal for Pentecostal-Charismatic Research* 5 (February 1999). No pages. Online: http://www.pctii.org/cyberj/cyberj5/alvarez.pdf.

Amstutz, Mark, and Peter Meilaender. "Public Policy and the Church: Spiritual Priorities." *The City* 4 (Spring 2011) 4–17.

Anderson, Robert Mapes. *Vision of the Disinherited: The Making of American Pentecostalism.* Peabody, MA: Hendrickson, 1979.

Awabdy, Mark A. *Immigrants and Innovative Law: Deuteronomy's Theological and Social Vision for the Ger.* FAT 2/67. Tübingen: Mohr Siebeck, 2014.

Azaransky, Sarah, ed. *Religion and Politics in America's Borderlands.* Lanham, MD: Lexington, 2013.

Badillo, David A. *Latinos and the New Immigrant Church.* Baltimore: Johns Hopkins University Press, 2006.

Baggio, Fabio. "The Migrant Ministry: A Constant Concern of the Catholic Church." *Asian Christian Review* 4, no. 2 (Winter 2010) 47–69.

Bird, Michael F. *Evangelical Theology: A Biblical and Systematic Introduction.* Grand Rapids: Zondervan, 2013.

Bouman, Stephen, and Ralston Deffenbaugh. *They Are Us: Lutherans and Immigration.* Minneapolis: Fortress, 2009.

Brueggemann, Walter. *The Prophetic Imagination.* 2nd ed. Minneapolis: Fortress, 2001.

Bureau of European and Eurasian Affairs. "U.S. Relations With the Holy See." *U.S. Department of State,* October 31, 2013. No Pages. Online: http://www.state.gov/r/pa/ei/bgn/3819.htm.

Burgueño, Fidencio. "Los Inmigrantes y el Desafío de la Iglesia." *El Evangelio* 61, no. 1 (2007) 4–5.

Busto, Rudiger V. "'In the Outer Boundaries': Pentecostalism, Politics, and Reies López Tijerina's Civic Activism." In *Latino Religions and Civic Activism in the United States*, edited by Espinosa et al., 65–75.

Butler, Anthea. "Arizona Is the Hispanic Alabama: Religious Opposition to Immigration Law May Hurt GOP Coalitions." *Religion Dispatches*, May 12, 2010. No pages. Online: http://www.religiondispatches.org/archive/politics/2528/arizona_is_the_hispanic_alabama.

Calvin, John. *Calvin's Commentaries*. Vol. 5. Translated by James Anderson. 1846. Reprint, Grand Rapids: Baker, 2003.

———. *Institutes of the Christian Religion*. Edited by John T. McNeill and translated by Ford Lewis Battles. 2 vols. LCC 20–21. Philadelphia: Westminster, 1960.

———. *Sermons on 2 Samuel: Chapters 1–13*. Translated by Douglas Kelly. Carlisle, PA: Banner of Truth, 1992.

Carey, Brycchan. "John Wesley's *Thoughts upon Slavery* and the Language of the Heart." *BJRL* 85, nos. 2–3 (2003) 269–84.

Carroll R., M. Daniel. "Blessing the Nations: Toward a Biblical Theology of Mission from Genesis." *BBR* 10, no. 1 (2000) 17–34.

———. *Christians at the Border: Immigration, the Church, and the Bible*. 2nd ed. Grand Rapids: Brazos, 2013.

———. "Diaspora and Mission in the Old Testament." In *Diaspora Missiology Compendium*, edited by Sadiri Joy Tira and Tetsunao Yamamori. Global Diaspora Network. Manila: LifeChange, forthcoming.

———. "Reading the Bible through Other Lenses: New Vistas from a Hispanic Diaspora Perspective." In *Global Voices: Reading the Bible in the Majority World*, edited by Craig S. Keener and M. Daniel Carroll R., 3–26. Peabody, MA: Hendrickson, 2012.

———. "Welcoming the Stranger: Toward a Theology of Immigration in Deuteronomy." In *For Our Good Always: Studies on the Message and Influence of Deuteronomy in Honor of Daniel I. Block*, edited by Jason S. DeRouchie et al., 441–61. Winona Lake, IN: Eisenbrauns, 2013.

Carson, D. A. "Systematic Theology and Biblical Theology." In *New Dictionary of Biblical Theology: Exploring the Unity & Diversity of Scripture*, edited by T. Desmond Alexander and Brian S. Rosner, 89–104. Downers Grove, IL: InterVarsity, 2000.

Castelo, Daniel. "Resident and Illegal Aliens." *Apuntes: Reflexiones teológicas desde el margen hispano* 23, no. 2 (2003) 65–77.

Chavez, Arturo. "Hispanic Ministry and Social Justice." In *Hispanic Ministry in the 21st Century: Present and Future*, edited by Hosffman Ospino, 155–71. Miami: Convivium, 2010.

Chestnut, J. Andrew. *Devoted to Death: Santa Muerte, the Skeleton Saint*. New York: Oxford University Press, 2012.

Chilcote, Paul W. *Recapturing the Wesleys' Vision: An Introduction to the Faith of John and Charles Wesley*. Downers Grove, IL: InterVarsity, 2004.

Cleary, Edward L., and Hannah W. Stewart-Gambino, eds. *Power, Politics, and Pentecostalism in Latin America*. Boulder, CO: Westview, 1998.

Collins, Kenneth J. "Twentieth-Century Interpretations of John Wesley's Aldersgate Experience: Coherence or Confusion?" *Wesleyan Theol J* 24 (1989) 18–31.

Commission on Theology and Church Relations. *Immigrants Among Us: A Lutheran Framework for Addressing Immigration Issues.* St. Louis: The Lutheran Church—Missouri Synod, 2013.

Conde-Frazier, Elizabeth. *Listen to the Children: Conversations with Immigrant Families/ Escuchemos a los niños: Conversaciones con familias inmigrantes.* Bilingual Edition. Valley Forge, PA: Judson Press, 2011.

Cornell, Deirdre. *Jesus Was a Migrant.* Maryknoll, NY: Orbis, 2014.

Cortés, Luis Jr. *De inmigrante a cuidadano: Cómo obtener o cambiar su estatus migratorio en Estados Unidos.* Serie Esperanza. New York: Atria, 2008.

Cruz, Gemma Tulud. "A New Way of Being Christian: The Contribution of Migrants to the Church." In *Contemporary Issues of Migration and Theology,* edited by Elaine Padilla and Peter C. Phan, 95–120. New York: Palgrave Macmillan, 2013.

Cuéllar, Gregory Lee. *Voices of Marginality: Exile and Return in Second Isaiah 40–55 and the Mexican Immigrant Experience.* American University Studies VII: Theology and Religion 271. New York: Peter Lang, 2008.

Culpepper, Raymond F. "The Hispanic Blessing." *Engage: A Journal for Church of God Leaders* 6, no. 2 (Spring 2010) 4–6. Online: http://digital.turn-page.com/i/53787.

Daniel, Ben. *Neighbor: Christian Encounters with "Illegal" Immigration.* Louisville: Westminster John Knox, 2010.

Davis, Cyprian, O.S.B. *The History of Black Catholics in the United States.* New York: Crossroad, 1990.

De La Torre, Miguel A. *Trails of Hope and Terror: Testimonies on Immigration.* Maryknoll, NY: Orbis, 2009.

De Leon, Victor. *The Silent Pentecostals: A Biographical History of the Pentecostal Movement among Hispanics in the Twentieth Century.* Taylors, SC: Faith, 1979.

del Campo, Ismael Martín. "Apostolic Assembly of the Faith in Christ Jesus." In *Los Evangélicos: Portraits of Latino Protestantism in the United States,* edited by Juan Martínez and Lindy Scott, 51–75. Eugene, OR: Wipf & Stock, 2009.

Elizondo, Virgilio. *Galilean Journey: The Mexican-American Promise.* Rev. ed. Maryknoll, NY: Orbis, 2000.

Espinosa, Gastón. "Latino Clergy and Churches in Faith-Based Political and Social Action in the United States." In *Latino Religions and Civic Activism in the United States,* edited by Gastón Espinosa et al., 279–304. Oxford: Oxford University Press, 2005.

———. "Latinos, Religion, and the American Presidency." In *Religion, Race, and the American Presidency,* edited by Gastón Espinosa, 231–74. Lanham, MD: Rowman & Littlefield, 2010.

———. "'Salvation and Transformation': Latino Evangelical Political Activism and the Struggle over Immigration Reform." In *Wading through Many Voices: Toward a Theology of Public Conversation,* edited by Harold Recinos, 133–51. Lanham, MD: Rowman & Littlefield, 2011.

Espinosa, Gastón, et al. "Introduction: U.S. Latino Religions and Faith-Based Political, Civic, and Social Action." In *Latino Religions and Civic Activism in the United States,* edited by Espinosa et al., 3–16. Oxford: Oxford University Press, 2005.

Espinosa, Gastón, et al., eds. *Latino Religions and Civic Activism in the United States.* Oxford: Oxford University Press, 2005.

Ferguson, Kathryn, et al. *Crossing with the Virgin: Stories from the Migrant Trail.* Tucson, AZ: University of Arizona Press, 2010.

BIBLIOGRAPHY

Fernandez, Eleazar S., and Fernando F. Segovia, eds. *A Dream Unfinished: Theological Reflections on America from the Margins*. Maryknoll, NY: Orbis, 2001.

Fiddian-Qasmiyeh, Elena, et al., eds. *The Oxford Handbook of Refugee and Forced Migration Studies*. Oxford: Oxford University Press, 2014.

Flores, Juan. *The Diaspora Strikes Back: Caribeño Tales of Learning and Turning*. New York: Routledge, 2009.

Garcia, Mario T., ed. *The Gospel of César Chávez: My Faith in Action*. Lanham, MD: Sheed & Ward, 2007.

The General Council of the Assemblies of God. "Statement on 'Immigration.'" *Assemblies of God*. No pages. Online: http://www.ag.org/top/about/immigration.cfm.

González, Justo L. *Santa Biblia: The Bible through Hispanic Eyes*. Nashville: Abingdon, 1996.

Groody, Daniel G., and Gioacchino Campese, eds. *A Promised Land, A Perilous Journey: Theological Perspectives on Migration*. Notre Dame: University of Notre Dame Press, 2008.

Gunter, Stephen W., et al. *Wesley and the Quadrilateral: Renewing the Conversation*. Nashville: Abingdon, 1997.

Hagan, Jacqueline María. *Migration Miracle: Faith, Hope, and Meaning on the Undocumented Journey*. Cambridge, MA: Harvard University Press, 2008.

Harper, Steve. *The Way to Heaven: The Gospel according to John Wesley*. Grand Rapids: Zondervan, 2003.

Herrera-Sobek, Maria. "A Farm Worker Hero and His Corridos (Ballads)." In *An American Leader: César E. Chávez*, edited by Alicia Marquez, 19–30. Los Angeles: Latino Museum of History, Art and Culture, 1999.

Hoffmeier, James K. *The Immigration Crisis: Immigrants, Aliens, and the Bible*. Wheaton, IL: Crossway, 2009.

Hynson, Leon O. *To Reform the Nation: Theological Foundations of Wesley's Ethics*. Grand Rapids: Zondervan, 1984.

Isasi-Díaz, Ada María, and Fernando F. Segovia, eds. *Hispanic/Latino Theology: Challenge and Promise*. Minneapolis: Fortress, 1996.

Jenkins, Philip. *The New Faces of Christianity: Believing the Bible in the Global South*. Oxford: Oxford University Press, 2006.

———. *The Next Christendom: The Coming of Global Christianity*. 3rd ed. Oxford: Oxford University Press, 2011.

Kaigwa, Mark. "D8A's 8 Lessons on the Future of African Tech from DEMO Africa 2013." *Appfrica*, November 27, 2013. No pages. Online: http://blog.appfrica.com/2013/11/27/8-lessons-future-african-tech-demo-africa-2013/.

Kennedy, John W. "Welcoming Immigrants: AG Helps Lead Compassionate Focus among Church Groups." *Assemblies of God*, February 27, 2014. No pages. Online: http://ag.org/top/News/index_articledetail.cfm?targetBay=c97d4d5c-a325-4921-9a9e-e9fbddd9cdce&ModID=2&Process=DisplayArticle&RSS_RSSContentID=27515&RSS_OriginatingChannelID=1184&RSS_OriginatingRSSFeedID=3359&RSS_Source=.

Kerwin, Donald, and Jill Marie Gerschutz, eds. *And You Welcomed Me: Migration and Catholic Social Teaching*. Lanham, MD: Lexington Books, 2009.

Kingdon, Robert M. "Calvinism and Social Welfare." *CTJ* 17 (1982) 212–30.

———. "Social Welfare in Calvin's Geneva." *AHR* 76, no. 1 (1971) 50–69.

Kinnaman, Gary. "Ready4Reform." No pages. Online: http://ready4reform.org/post/67385357260/gary-as-we-sit-on-our-political-hands-more-people.

Knighton, Tess, and Álvaro Torrente, eds. *Devotional Music in the Iberian World, 1450–1800: The Villancico and Related Genres*. Aldershot, Hampshire: Ashgate, 2007.

Knox, John. *The Works of John Knox*. 6 vols. Edited by David Laing. Eugene, OR: Wipf & Stock, 2004.

Kolb, Robert, and Timothy Wengert, eds. *The Book of Concord: The Confessions of the Evangelical Lutheran Church*. Minneapolis: Fortress, 2000.

Laird, Paul R. *Towards a History of the Spanish Villancico*. Detroit Studies in Musicology; Studies in Music 19. Warren, MI: Harmonie Park, 1997.

Lalive d'Epinay, Christian. *Haven of the Masses: A Study of the Pentecostal Movement in Chile*. Translated by Marjorie Sandle. World Studies of Churches in Mission. London: Lutterworth, 1969.

Larsen, Timothy. "Defining and Locating Evangelicalism." In *The Cambridge Companion to Evangelical Theology*, edited by Timothy Larsen and Daniel J. Treier, 1–14. Cambridge: Cambridge University Press, 2007.

Libro de Liturgia y Cántico. N.p.: Augsburg Fortress, 1998.

Lindberg, Carter. *The European Reformations*. Oxford: Blackwell, 1996.

Lohse, Bernard. *Martin Luther's Theology: Its Historical and Systematic Development*. Minneapolis: Fortress, 1999.

Lovin, Robin W. "Moral Theology." In *The Oxford Handbook of Methodist Studies,* edited by William J. Abraham and James E. Kirby, 647–61. New York: Oxford University Press, 2009.

Lozada, Francisco Jr., and Fernando F. Segovia, eds. *Latino/a Biblical Hermeneutics: Problematics, Objectives, Strategies*. SemeiaST 68. Atlanta: SBL Press, 2014.

Luther, Martin. "Christmas Day." In *The Complete Sermons of Martin Luther*, edited by John Nicolas Lenker and translated by Geo. H. Trabert, 134–60. Vol. 1/1. Grand Rapids: Baker, 2000.

———. *Luther's Works*. American ed. 55 vols. Edited by Jaroslav Pelikan and Helmut T. Lehman. Philadelphia: Fortress; St. Louis: Concordia, 1955–1986.

Machado, Daisy L. *Of Borders and Margins: Hispanic Disciples in Texas, 1888–1945*. American Academy of Religion Academy Series. Oxford: Oxford University Press, 2003.

Maddox, Randy L., ed. *Responsible Grace: John Wesley's Practical Theology*. Nashville: Kingswood, 1994.

Magallanes, Hugo. "Wesleyan Ethics." In *Dictionary of Scripture and Ethics*, edited by Joel B. Green et al., 833–36. Grand Rapids: Baker, 2011.

Marcial, Ángel. "Hispanos y la Inmigración." *Engage: A Journal for Church of God Leaders* 6, no. 2 (2010) 17–19.

Matters, Michael D. "The Sanctuary Movement, 1980–1988: An Organizational Analysis of Structures and Cultures." PhD diss., University of Illinois at Chicago, 1994.

McDermott, Gerald R., ed. *The Oxford Handbook of Evangelical Theology*. Oxford: Oxford University Press, 2010.

McGrath, Alister E. "Faith and Tradition." In *The Oxford Handbook of Evangelical Theology*, edited by McDermott, 81–95. Oxford: Oxford University Press, 2010.

McKee, Elsie Anne. "The Character and Significance of John Calvin's Teaching on Social and Economic Issues." In *John Calvin Rediscovered: The Impact of His Social and Economic Thought*, edited by Edward Dommen and James D. Bratt, 3–24. PTSSRTH. Louisville: Westminster John Knox, 2007.

————. *Diakonia in the Classical Reformed Tradition and Today*. Grand Rapids: Eerdmans, 1989.

————. *John Calvin on the Diaconate and Liturgical Almsgiving*. Geneva: Droz, 1984.

Meilaender, Peter C. "Immigration: Citizens and Strangers." *First Things* 173 (2007) 10–12.

————. *Toward a Theory of Immigration*. New York: Palgrave, 2001.

Nanko-Fernández, Carmen. *Theologizing en Espanglish: Context, Community and Ministry*. Maryknoll, NY: Orbis, 2010.

Naphy, William G. "Calvin's Church in Geneva: Constructed or Gathered? Local or Foreign? French or Swiss?" In *Calvin and His Influence, 1509–2009*, edited by Irena Backus and Philip Benedict, 102–18. Oxford: Oxford University Press, 2011.

————. "Calvin's Geneva." In *The Cambridge Companion to John Calvin*, edited by Donald K. McKim, 25–37. Cambridge: Cambridge University Press, 2004.

Naselli, Andrew David, and Collin Hansen, eds. *Four Views on the Spectrum of Evangelicalism*. Counterpoints. Grand Rapids: Zondervan, 2011.

Nguyen, vanThanh, and John M. Prior, eds. *God's People on the Move: Biblical and Global Perspectives on Migration and Mission*. Eugene, OR: Pickwick, 2014.

Noll, Mark. "What is 'Evangelical'?" In *The Oxford Handbook of Evangelical Theology*, edited by McDermott, 19–32.

O'Dowd, Peter. "Some Latinos Support Arizona's New Immigration Law." *NPR*, May 25, 2010. No pages. Online: http://www.npr.org/templates/story/story.php?storyId=127105843.

Oberman, Heiko A. *The Two Reformations: The Journey from the Last Days to the New World*. Edited by Donald Weinstein. New Haven, CT: Yale University Press, 2003.

Ogletree, Thomas W. *The Use of the Bible in Christian Ethics*. Louisville: Westminster John Knox, 2003.

Olson, Jeannine E. *Calvin and Social Welfare: Deacons and the Bourse française*. London: Associated University Press, 1989.

Ott, Craig. "Diaspora and Relocation as Divine Impetus for Witness in the Early Church." In *Diaspora Missiology: Theory, Methodology, and Practice*, edited by Enoch Wan, 73–94. Portland: Institute of Diaspora Studies, 2011.

Ottati, Douglas F. "What Reformed Theology in a Calvinist Key Brings to Conversations about Justice." *Political Theology* 10, no. 3 (2009) 447–69.

Outler, Albert C. "The Wesleyan Quadrilateral in Wesley." *Wesleyan Theol J* 20, no. 1 (1985) 7–18.

Padilla, Elaine, and Peter C. Phan, eds. *Theology of Migration in the Abrahamic Religions*. Christianities of the World. New York: Palgrave Macmillan, 2014.

Parker, T. H. L. *John Calvin: A Biography*. Louisville: Westminster John Knox, 2007.

Passel, Jeffrey S., and D'Vera Cohn. "Unauthorized Immigrant Totals Rise in 7 States, Fall in 14: Decline in Those From Mexico Fuels Most State Decreases." *Pew Research Center*, November 18, 2014. Online: http://www.pewhispanic.org/files/2014/11/2014-11-18_unauthorized-immigration.pdf.

Rah, Soong-Chan. *The Next Evangelicalism: Freeing the Church from Western Cultural Captivity*. Downers Grove, IL: InterVarsity, 2009.

Ramírez, Daniel. "Borderlands Praxis: The Immigrant Experience in Latino Pentecostal Churches." *JAAR* 67, no. 3 (1999) 573–96.

————. "Call Me 'Bitter': Life and Death in the Diasporic Borderland and the Challenges/Opportunities for *Norteamericano* Churches." *Perspectivas/Occasional Papers* (Fall 2007) 39–66.

————. "Divino Compañero del Camino: The Stakes for Latino Pentecostal Theology in Pentecostalism's Second Century." In *The Many Faces of Global Pentecostalism*, edited by Harold D. Hunter and Neil Ormerod, 199–217. Cleveland, TN: CPT Press, 2013.

————. "Open Letter to Rev. Representative Steve Montenegro." April 23, 2010. No pages. Online: http://www.apostolicfriendsforum.com/showthread.php?p=910094.

————. "Public Lives in American Hispanic Churches: Expanding the Paradigm." In *Latino Religions and Civic Activism in the United States*, edited by Espinosa et al., 177–95. Oxford: Oxford University Press, 2005.

Ratzinger, Josef Cardinal. *Milestones: Memoirs, 1927–1977*. San Francisco: Ignatius, 1998.

Ríos, Elizabeth D. "The Ladies Are Warriors: Latina Pentecostalism and Faith-based Activism in New York City." In *Latino Religions and Civic Activism in the United States*, edited by Gaston Espinosa et al., 197–217. Oxford: Oxford University Press, 2005.

Rivera-Pagán, Luis N. "Pentecostal Transformation in Latin America." In *Twentieth-Century Global Christianity*, edited by Mary Farrell Bednarowski, 190–210. Vol. 7 of *A People's History of Christianity*. Edited by Denis R. Janz. Minneapolis: Fortress, 2010.

Rodríguez, Luis Rivera. "Toward a Diaspora Hermeneutics (Hispanic North America)." In *Character Ethics and the Old Testament: Moral Dimensions of Scripture*, edited by M. Daniel Carroll R. and Jacqueline E. Lapsley, 169–89. Louisville: Westminster John Knox, 2007.

Rodriguez, Samuel. *The Lamb's Agenda: Why Jesus Is Calling You to a Life of Righteousness and Justice*. Nashville: Thomas Nelson, 2013.

Rose, Amanda. *Showdown in the Sonoran Desert: Religion, Law, and the Immigration Controversy*. New York: Oxford University Press, 2012.

Ruiz, Jean-Pierre. *Reading from the Edges: The Bible and People on the Move*. Maryknoll, NY: Orbis, 2011.

Salguero, Gabriel. "An Open Letter to Governor Brewer of Arizona." *Sojourners*, April 22, 2010. No Pages. Online: http://sojo.net/blogs/2010/04/22/open-letter-governor-brewer-arizona.

Sánchez M., Leopoldo A. "The Human Face of Justice: Reclaiming the Neighbor in Law, Vocation, and Justice Talk." *Concordia Journal* 39, no. 2 (2013) 117–32.

————. "Misión e inmigración: Pedagogía para trabajar entre los inmigrantes." *Missio Apostolica* 16, no. 1 (2008) 70–74.

Sassen, Saskia. *Globalization and Its Discontents: Essays on the New Mobility of People and Money*. New York: The New Press, 1998.

Schweikert, Anahid. "A Voice for Immigrants." *Charisma* 36, no. 3 (2010). No pages. Online: http://www.charismamag.com/site-archives/570-news/featured-news/12092-a-voice-for-immigrants.

Selderhuis, Herman J. *John Calvin: A Pilgrim's Life*. Translated by Albert Gootjes. Downers Grove, IL: IVP Academic, 2009.

Snyder, Howard A. *The Radical Wesley and Patterns for Church Renewal*. Eugene, OR: Wipf & Stock, 1996.

Solana, Kimber. "Illegal Immigrants Give Billions to Medicare, Social Security With No Hope of Benefit." *The Medicare Newsgroup*, January 7, 2013. No pages. Online: http://www.medicarenewsgroup.com/context/understanding-medicare-blog/understanding-medicare-blog/2013/01/07/illegal-immigrants-give-billions-to-medicare-social-security-with-no-hope-of-benefit.

Soliván, Samuel. "Sources of Hispanic/Latino American Theology: A Pentecostal Perspective." In *Hispanic/Latino Theology: Challenge and Promise*, edited by Ada María Isasi-Díaz and Fernando F. Segovia, 134–50. Minneapolis: Fortress, 1996.

———. *The Spirit, Pathos and Liberation: Toward an Hispanic Pentecostal Theology.* Sheffield: Sheffield Academic, 1998.

Streeter, Kurt. "Spreading the Pentecostal Spirit." *Los Angeles Times*, February 2, 2014. No pages. Online: http://www.latimes.com/local/la-me-latino-pentecostal-20140202, 0,2060392.story#ixzz2ze38Jn1p.

Suárez-Orozco, Marcelo M. "The Remittance Hole." *Americas Quarterly* (Spring 2009) 85–89. Online: http://icy.gseis.ucla.edu/articles/remittance-hole-1.pdf.

Thorsen, Don. *The Wesleyan Quadrilateral: Scripture, Tradition, Reason, and Experience as a Model of Evangelical Theology.* Lexington, KY: Emeth, 2005.

Three Sonorans. "Who Is Steve Montenegro?" *Three Sonorans News & Analysis*, July 14, 2010. No pages. Online: https://threesonorans.com/2010/07/14/who-is-steve-montenegro-video/.

TMS Ruge. "Message to Davos: Don't Forget Africa." *CNN*, January 26, 2011. No pages. Online: https://www.linkedin.com/in/tmsruge.

United Nations. "International Migration 2013." No Pages. Online: http://www.un.org/en/development/desa/population/migration/publications/wallchart/docs/wallchart2013.pdf.

van't Spijker, Willem. "Bucer's Influence on Calvin: Church and Community." In *Martin Bucer: Reforming Church and Community*, edited by D. F. Wright, 32–44. Cambridge: Cambridge University Press, 1994.

Vatican Documents and Other Official Pronouncements:

    Benedict XVI. *Caritas in Veritate.* June 29, 2009. No pages. Online: http://www.vatican.va/holy_father/benedict_xvi/encyclicals/documents/hf_ben-xvi_enc_20090629_caritas-in-veritate_en.html.

    ———. "Homily." Washington Nationals Stadium, Washington DC, April 17, 2008. No pages. Online: http://www.vatican.va/holy_father/benedict_xvi/homilies/2008/documents/hf_ben-xvi_hom_20080417_washington-stadium_en.html.

    ———. "Homily." Yankee Stadium, Bronx, New York, April 20, 2008. No pages. Online: http://www.vatican.va/holy_father/benedict_xvi/homilies/2008/documents/hf_ben-xvi_hom_20080420_yankee-stadium-ny_en.html.

    ———. "Interview of the Holy Father Benedict XVI during the Flight to the United States of America." April 15, 2008. No pages. Online: http://www.vatican.va/holy_father/benedict_xvi/speeches/2008/april/documents/hf_ben-xvi_spe_20080415_intervista-usa_en.html.

    ———. "Meeting with Young People and Seminarians." Saint Joseph Seminary, Yonkers, New York, April 19, 2008. No pages. Online: http://www.vatican.va/holy_father/benedict_xvi/speeches/2008/april/documents/hf_ben-xvi_spe_20080419_st-joseph-seminary_en.html.

    ———. "Migrations: Pilgrimage of Faith and Hope." Message for the 99th World Day of Migrants and Refugees (2013). October 12, 2012. No pages. Online: http://www.vatican.va/holy_father/benedict_xvi/messages/migration/documents/hf_ben-xvi_mes_20121012_world-migrants-day_en.html.

    ———. "One Human Family." Message for the 97th World Day of Migrants and Refugees (2011). September 27, 2010. No pages. Online: http://www.vatican.